Law and TV Series

Art and Law

Volumes published in this Brill Research Perspectives title are listed at *brill.com/rpal*

Law and TV Series

By

Adam Andrzejewski and Mateusz Salwa

BRILL

LEIDEN | BOSTON

This paperback book edition is simultaneously published as issue 2.2 (2018) of *Art and Law*,
DOI:10.1163/24684309-12340004.

Library of Congress Control Number: 2018952249

Typeface for the Latin, Greek, and Cyrillic scripts: "Brill". See and download: brill.com/brill-typeface.

ISBN 978-90-04-38787-4 (paperback)
ISBN 978-90-04-38788-1 (e-book)

This book is printed on acid-free paper and produced in a sustainable manner.

Contents

Law and TV Series

Adam Andrzejewski
University of Warsaw, Poland
a.andrzejewski@uw.edu.pl

Mateusz Salwa
University of Warsaw, Poland
mateusz.salwa@uw.edu.pl

Abstract

The aim of the article is to analyse seriality from the point of view of philosophical aesthetics. Such an approach reveals that seriality has a normative character that is often overlooked by other disciplines. Seriality is unanimously considered to be one of the most characteristic traits of contemporary popular culture, but the field where it currently comes to the foreground is TV series. They have been studied within media theory and cultural studies for quite a long time, but they have been analysed mainly in terms of their production, distribution, and consumption across various and changing social contexts. Aiming to show how philosophy may contribute to "seriality studies", the authors follow the agenda of philosophical aesthetics and conceive of seriality as a factor which defines the structure of TV series, their aesthetic properties, as well as their modes of reception. They claim that seriality is normative as it is possible to indicate what features a television show has to have in order to be a serial show as well as the manner in which it should be watched if it is to be experienced as a serial work.

Keywords

normativity – TV series – aesthetics – ontology – seriality

 | DOI:10.1163/9789004387881_002

1 Introduction: Law, TV Series and Aesthetics

> […] how would we read a piece of a series, if the whole of the series remained unknown to us?
>
> UMBERTO ECO

There is no doubt that there is a close relationship between law and TV series. Given that the latter are currently a substantial part of the media market and entertainment, legal issues are crucial for their production, distribution, and consumption. Legal vicissitudes are also an important subject of TV series as many of them may be classified as belonging to the legal genre (e.g. *Silk, The Good Fight, Damages, Suits, The Good Wife, Fearless* or *The Honourable Woman*).

If one were to focus on this aspect of serial TV shows, one could either analyse how legal issues and/or lawyers are represented in them or treat the dramas as inspiring examples that can be referred to in discussions on specific law problems. In both cases TV series would be conceived of as illustrations, either of the manner in which law and lawyers are pictured in media, providing significant material for analyses of how a society imagines the culture of law, or as epitomes of certain issues crucial for theory or philosophy of law.[1]

Certainly, the above topics are important and fruitfully looked into by media theorists and cultural studies scholars, nevertheless, they do not quite fit the agenda of philosophical aesthetics, i.e. the perspective we are going to assume throughout our paper, as they do not foster looking at TV series as specific kinds of artefacts. In fact, interpreted in the two manners suggested above, TV series do not differ from other shows or films.

Philosophical aesthetics, as we understand it, is a subfield of philosophy which is interested in (1) art and other artefacts which have aesthetic properties, (2) natural and human environments in terms of their aesthetic properties, (3) the everyday as a sphere where aesthetic choices are made and aesthetic practices take place, and (4) aesthetic experiences and all their articulations and expressions. Philosophical aesthetics is based on concept analysis and aims at offering a theory which would allow one to describe various phenomena taking place *hic et nunc* within the art world and outside of it. While it does not want to overlook "empirical" data, its ambition is to create a theory or suggest solutions useful in broader contexts than just a narrow set of works or phenomena that were subject to scrutiny.

---

1 On that topic see e.g. Asimow (2009), Erickson (2009), Robson and Schulz (2016), Villez (2009); the philosophical significance of TV shows is briefly discussed in section 2.3.

One could argue that it is possible to relate law to TV series via aesthetics as is being done by more and more numerous attempts at approaching law from an aesthetic point of view.[2] Yet, in all probability, even in such a case one would not succeed in showing the aesthetic specificity of TV series. One could still suggest that law may be linked to aesthetics if we understand the former not as a set of rules governing human behaviour, but as a set of general principles in force within aesthetics. The idea that there are aesthetic laws is, however, highly debatable.[3] It did occur in the past—either consciously, mainly as censorship practices, or unconsciously in aesthetic theories which—as Weitz (1956) remarks—were expressions of their proponents' tastes and aimed at defining what art was or what good art was like.

In spite of our claim that there exist no aesthetic laws analogous to the general laws discussed in sciences, we do believe that it is possible to claim that there are aesthetic laws provided that they are identified with aesthetic norms. Therefore, we contend that one may reasonably state that aesthetics is normative in a number of ways, i.e. that there are norms that have to be fulfilled by an object if it is to be a painting, a sculpture, or a TV series. What is more, it is our belief that if we are to analyse TV series from an aesthetic point of view in order to offer new insights different from those offered by other disciplines, we have to focus on nothing other than aesthetic norms that define the structure as well as the reception of TV series.

The perspective we are going to assume below differs from the approaches that may be encountered in media or culture studies in that its scope is more general than theirs. If we refer to certain TV series, we will do it only for the sake of the argument and treat them as mere "visualizations". Of course, media theory and culture studies are not merely idiographic, yet they hardly ever offer broad generalizations that go beyond the level of the TV genre (e.g. legal drama) or of a specific broadcaster (e.g. HBO or American television). Nor do scholars working in media and culture studies seem to be particularly interested in aesthetic issues as conceived of by philosophical aesthetics. More often than not, they equate aesthetics with criticism, which makes them approach it rather cautiously.

We are going to refer to research done by specialists in other fields, but at the same time we will try to answer the following question—"what can philosophy tell us about TV series?" We believe that the perspective offered by

2 On that topic see e.g. Ben Dor (2012), Carneiro (2011), Gearey (2001), Morgan (2007).

3 The existence of laws was discussed by, among others, Mary Mothersill (1984), as well as by exponents of neuro-aesthetics or of evolutionary aesthetics.

philosophical aesthetics allows one to look differently at the issue which is, beyond any doubt, crucial for TV series, i.e. seriality. We agree that:

> Regardless of their circumstances of production, distribution, or reception, serials share a distinctive narrative form, one recognized by their viewers around the world. [...] Whether set in a middle-class American suburb, a Welsh village, nineteenth-century Rio, or the sacred time and place of Hindu myth, television serials are linked—in the way they are constructed, broadcast and watched—by their distinctive serial narrational structure.
>
> ALLEN 2001: 16

The distinctiveness of TV series lies in the fact that, contrary to other television formats, they are defined by a specific kind of relationship: (1) between the parts (episodes); (2) between the parts and the whole (the TV series) as well as (3) the parts and the series as a whole (the season). Seriality is ontologically and aesthetically significant and—as we claim—the ontology of TV series determines their aesthetic properties.[4] Hence, if we are to approach these kinds of shows and norms (laws) from the standpoint of philosophical aesthetics, we have to analyse seriality.

We are well aware that seriality is, metaphorically speaking, the meeting point of production, distribution, and consumption and that it largely stems from economic motives. Nevertheless, we think that it is the factor that makes TV series interesting for philosophical aesthetics. Thus, by analysing them we intend to go beyond the traditional boundaries of aesthetics, which still remains a philosophy of arts (mainly high ones).[5]

This is one of the reasons why we will give so much importance to references to art. There are ongoing debates in television aesthetics on the artistic status of TV series, all the more now that many of them are artified as they are imbued with more and more properties that are usually highly appreciated in artworks.[6] Even if our aim is not to decide whether serial dramas are works of art, we follow those discussions in so far as we use what philosophical

4 Given that we want to focus on seriality, we are not interested in whether the ontology of TV series is similar to or different from the ontology of cinematic films—on that topic see e.g. Shuster (2017), Bandirali and Terrone (2012).

5 In this respect our intention is to modestly follow in the footsteps of e.g. Carroll (1998) or Welsch (1997).

6 On artification see Naukkarinen (2012), Saito (2012), Leddy (2012). See also Andrzejewski (2015).

aesthetics says about art—especially on the ontology of art and the reception of art—in order to better understand seriality.[7]

Our paper is structured as follows: Starting from §2 we introduce and analyse the concept of seriality as it is embodied in culture and the arts. Next, in §3, the relationship between authority, normativity, and philosophical aesthetics is drawn and defended. It is suggested that in philosophical aesthetics there are two norms: the categorial norm and the aesthetic norm. §4 provides an overview of so-called television aesthetics as well as a summary of the major points regarding the nature of Quality TV and Complex TV. In the next sections, §5 and §6, the ontology and aesthetics of TV series are presented and linked to the issues of normativity. In the concluding section (§7), the summary of our argument is stated along with refutations of possible objections.

2 Seriality in Art and Culture

2.1 *Seriality in Art: "Opałka 1965/1-∞"*

Roman Opałka (1931–2011) was one of the most renowned Polish contemporary painters. He was mostly famous for his series of *Counted Paintings* (the title of the project as a whole was *Opałka 1965/1-∞*) which he began to create in 1965 by painting the number "1" in the upper left corner of a canvas (*Roman Opalka* 1999). The series consists of numerous canvases on which the painter consistently and minutely put down subsequent numbers until his death. All the pictures (which, taken separately, are called *Details*) have the same dimensions just as all the white numbers written throughout the years are of the same tiny size. Originally, all the paintings were supposed to be black, but in 1972 Opałka decided that every new picture would be brighter by 1% than the previous one and that at some point he would be inevitably forced to put white numbers on white background. The process of fading out can also be seen in every single painting, because Opałka would write the numbers without adding paint to the brush as long as they remained visible. In 1968 he started recording his voice while he pronounced the numbers he was painting. It is noteworthy that the artist calculated what number he would be able to arrive at during his lifetime (7777777), which he did not, however, manage to achieve. Opałka himself interpreted his work as a recording of the passage of time.

It is usually underlined that Opałka's work is exceptional in conceptual as well as formal terms. In fact, it is hardly possible to find an equally obsessive

7 An analogous approach may be found e.g. in environmental aesthetics, another example of "aesthetics beyond aesthetics" (Carlson 1999).

artistic project conveying such a deep existential message which would be realized in a comparably minimalist form. Indeed, *Opałka 1965/1-∞* is "just" a series of monochromes changing in brightness covered with scrip which, seen from a distance, creates a pulsing rhythm of white spots. Such a formalistic-iconological approach tends, however, to overlook what is really crucial for the project as a whole, namely its serial aspect, which is noteworthy as Opałka's serial strategy has ontological and aesthetic consequences.

His work vertiginously combines repetition, serialization, and temporal dilatation, i.e. three factor which, taken together, define the aesthetics of seriality (Aprile 2010: 13, Casetti 1984). Every *Detail* presents the same motif, a series of numbers consisting of iterated digits; every painting occupies a predefined place in the series to which it belongs and as such it directs the beholder's attention to the previous (past) picture(s) as well as to the subsequent (future) one(s). The same may be said about the numbers on the canvases which form "intra-picture" mathematical sequences. Finally, the whole project may be seen—as was suggest by the painter himself—as a recording of the time that passed from the moment the project was initiated, wherein every single *Detail* may be perceived individually as a spatial recording of the time required by its creation.

Ontologically speaking, *Opałka 1965/1-∞* is a set of pictures that were sequentially painted between 1965 and 2011. As long as the artist was alive, the set was open in the sense that he kept adding new pictures to the existing ones. Only when the project was finished due to his death, was the set (series) closed. In this sense, in so far as the series consists of single paintings, it is ontologically "preceded" by them. Yet, *Opałka 1965/1-∞* is not simply a whole created by adding new paintings, but a structure or a composition that defines the place of all the paintings it consists of. Hence, the project as a whole is ontologically prior to the pictures. This ontological hierarchy characterizes not only *Opałka 1965/1-∞* as a closed set, but it also characterized the project while it was still going on and heading toward infinity, i.e. when there were still paintings to be made.

The serial ontology of Opałka's work is closely related to its aesthetic qualities. The *Details* may be appreciated together as *Opałka 1965/1-∞* (interestingly, in 2003 the artist decided that they would be exhibited together in an octagonal space) or individually at exhibitions and in private collections. Despite having an unquestionable visual appeal and that they may be aesthetically appreciated and interpreted as finished artworks containing finished mathematical series, in order to make their aesthetic appreciation and interpretation, if not more adequate, then at least fuller or more rewarding, one should take into account the whole project. Only such an approach makes it possible to see

Opałka 1965/1-∞ and thus all its parts as a painterly narration about time passing by as well as about consciousness of the inevitable. In this respect there is little difference between appreciating Opałka's project when it was still in progress and appreciating it after his death.

In other words, one has to recognize and acknowledge the ontological priority of *Opałka 1965/1-∞* as a whole. As a result, one notices that the paintings are not closed units linked to one another by their formal resemblance or subject, but that they are open in so far as they refer to the previous and following elements of the series as well as to the series as a whole.

Thanks to the conceptual dimension of his project and its minimalist form, Opałka introduced the aesthetics of seriality to a realm of modern art still ruled by the myth of originality (Krauss 1986). Consequently, seriality, which used to be considered a negation of uniqueness and unrepeatability, became original—losing its principal characteristic decried by those who associated it with mass culture. This was the only way that seriality could prove to be noble enough to be studied by traditional aesthetics, which tended to ignore mass art. It is no wonder that so much attention was paid to the serial character of minimal art.[8]

2.2 *Cultural Seriality*

There is no need to quote the notorious criticisms of cultural industry and their refutations. Hostility towards seriality, as is well known, largely stemmed from the fact that it was identified with mechanical reproduction aimed at reducing creative costs and at maximizing the income from mass consumption. The paradigm of seriality was found mainly in serial production of goods of poor quality.[9]

The change in the general attitude observable in academia over the past decades was partly due to the fact that the aesthetic potential of seriality has finally been noticed. Seriality no longer amounts to an eternal return of the same but is seen more as a "difference and repetition", to use Deleuze's (2004) felicitous expression. It also became obvious that the idea that culture is defined by the principle of unrepeatability is an expression of contingent, historical assumptions backed by an ideology.

Reproducibility, as described by Walter Benjamin (2008) in relation to changes in 19th-century culture, is not literally or even metaphorically mechanical and is much older than the invention of the press and film, i.e. the

8 See e.g. Dyer (2011), Slowinska (2014: 62–72), Zhou (2015).

9 That being said, serial production was also characteristic for high quality industrial design, e.g. Bauhaus projects.

two spheres in which modern seriality came to the foreground. The practice of reproducing works of art, e.g. copying ancient sculpture or creating allographic works (Goodman 1968), has been known to people for a very long time, as Benjamin himself shows. Even such noble aesthetic categories as *mimesis, emulation*, or the dialectic of tradition and innovation may be interpreted in terms of seriality. Recognizing that so-called high art is based on repetition allows one to notice that even so-called low art, e.g. folklore, cannot be reductively seen as solely reproducing models either taken from high art or created autonomously, because it is loaded with innovation which very often passes unnoticed. Putting it in the broadest possible terms, seriality is typical of every institutionalized practice. Even the most innovatory and revolutionary solutions perforce have to refer to, i.e. to repeat in a certain measure, solutions that are considered canonical.

All this, however, does not change the fact that in the 20th century cultural seriality gained in importance to such an extent that it effectively changed social and cultural reality, as Benjamin wrote. As the editors of the volume "Zeitschrift für Medienwissenschaften", dedicated to serial production, justly state: "Serial production, structures and aesthetics of seriality and serials […] are an excellent sign of modernity" (Beil et al. 2012: 10). The ground for the career of seriality was offered not only by the logic of late capitalism that defined forms and genres of newspapers, films, and TV formats, but also by the interests of various artists, Opałka being one of them. Serial solutions were equally used by artists who, like Andy Warhol, flirted with the world of mass consumption, by those who commented upon it, while keeping a safe distance from it, as well as by those who tried to save avant-garde autonomy—like composers creating serial music, i.e. music based on the repetition of a series of sound patterns. Seriality also became conspicuous thanks to such practices as quotation, *pastiche*, remix, or adaptation, which were particularly developed in the second half the 20th century.[10]

The constantly growing interest in seriality finds its expression in research on the history of serial forms, especially those typical of popular culture (from *The Pickwick's Papers*, 19th-century *feuilletons*, serial cinema, radio dramas, and comic books, to soap opera and quality TV series)[11] as well as on serial

10 On these topics see Klein and Palmer (2016), Verevis (2006), Wells-Lassagne (2017).

11 E.g. Allen and van der Berg (2014), Belphégore (2016), Greif, Lehnert, and Meywirth (2015), Kelleter (2012, 2017), Schleich and Nesselhauf (2016), Letourneux (2017).

aspects of such fields as scientific research, education, pornography or computer games, to name just a few.[12]

Today it is unanimously accepted that an "aesthetics of repetition" (Calabrese 1984) exists and that it contradicts the romantic aesthetics based on the idea of uniqueness and singularity of the work of art (Aprile 2010: 10). Even if seriality shapes different contemporary arts and practices, the field where it currently has the largest cultural impact is, beyond any doubt, TV series.[13]

2.3 *Studying TV Series*

As Milly Buonanno (2002) remarks, seriality is usually associated with television these days. Nevertheless, it may be conceived of in more general terms, even more broadly than the approaches quoted above. "We cannot be but serial"—Buonanno reiterates in her book. What makes our everyday existence stable and predictable, and hence possible at all, is the fact that we repeat the same gestures, do the same things, meet the same people, go to the same places (Bonazzi 2001). Our social performances would not have been successful, had they not been rooted in social bases which are enacted again and again. In other words, our everyday seriality lets us think that our social world is coherent and that we know how to act in it.

The factor that defined everyday seriality in the second half of the 20th century and at the beginning of the 21st century was television. TV series had—and still have even if to a somewhat lesser extent—their share in it. Broadcasted at a certain hour of the day, evening or night, repeating well-known forms (formats), conveying more or less expected meanings, they used to structure the TV flow (Grasso 2007: 18). At the same time, they imposed a rhythm onto their viewers who had to submit to the broadcasters' schedules, which gave a ritualistic shade to the act of watching a TV series.[14]

It explains why much more attention has been recently devoted to TV series than to other serial works. TV seriality has become so popular that something like a new discipline has emerged—"seriality studies".[15] The number of articles

12 On these topics see Denson and Jahn-Sundman (2013), "History of Science" (2010), Raimond, Ali, and England (2014), Schaschek (2013).

13 See e.g. texts by Mag Uidhir (2013), Pratt (2013), and Cook (2013).

14 Today it is only one possible model (Lotz 2014), but it still seems to be relevant in so far as it is treated as a point of reference, at least whenever TV series are discussed.

15 See e.g. http://heymancenter.org/events/the-new-seriality-studies; It should be underlined that TV series are discussed not only by journals generally dedicated to film and television studies, but also by periodicals specialized in this topic, e.g. "Journal of Serial Narration on Television", "Series. International Journal of TV Serial Narratives", "TV/Series"; at least three recent major research projects that focused on seriality may be mentioned here: "Popular Seriality. Aesthetics and Practice" (http://www.popularseriality

and books analysing specific TV series in various ways is far too vast to be taken into account. This trend is reinforced by the growing number of TV series that are produced every year, even if the academic discourse is dominated by American production, mainly TV series regarded as examples of "quality TV" that are supposed to define the "standard of taste" at the expense of "invisible television" (Mills 2010).

Despite TV series being researched from various perspectives—from the opening credits to the language spoken by the protagonists—the majority of analyses follow the approaches rooted in media and culture studies.

As a consequence, stress is placed on factors determining production, distribution, and consumption of TV series as well as on their content, i.e. the meanings which are coded and decoded in various manners. There are, then, lots of discussions over identity, gender, ethnicity, minorities, social exclusion and injustice, memory, etc. Such a research focus favours doing case studies of specific TV series, genres and formats, themes, single motifs, aesthetic qualities, and finally management strategies of broadcasters.

Special attention should be paid to philosophical interpretations of TV series which are treated as a sort of "pop-sophy", conceived of as an "intersection of philosophical reflection and mass culture",[16] which reflects the general idea that television is a medium which is either a useful tool for presenting philosophical issues or is a source of good illustrations of philosophical issues.[17] TV series are then treated as case studies that are good points of departure for debates on more general problems.[18] It is then believed that TV series deserve a philosophical interpretation because "they are today an art which goes deep into human nature" and that "the most interesting TV series are capable of creating significant philosophical discourses which help us to better understand the world we have been living in as well as forms of our existence" (Bandirali and Terrone 2012: 10).

The abovementioned approaches necessarily take into account the serial aspect of TV series, nevertheless they treat it as a rather technical issue which has its cultural consequences as far as it is a means of ideological power and as a specific narrative structure which determines the way meanings are coded

.de), "Innovation Strategies for Research on TV Serial Narratives" (http://researchseries.squarespace.com), "Serial Narration on Television" (https://www.uni-saarland.de/lehrstuhl/solte-gresser/forschung/serial-narration/home.html).

16 Quoted from: http://www.popsophia.it [last accessed: 03/29/18].

17 Chaplin (2017), Watson and Arp (2011).

18 Such an approach is expressed by the series *Popculture and Philosophy*. More than a hundred volumes have been published since 2000 and more or less thirty of them are devoted to TV series.

and decoded. It is also seriality that is very often treated as the quality criterion. Therefore, if it is believed that certain TV series may be highly prized as works of art that replace "good literature", it is so because of their serial character which justifies the claim that "a TV series is an art that conceals its artistic character" and that, nevertheless, it belongs to "the romantic order of aesthetics" (Grasso 2007: x).

Not only do series studies successfully reveal the cultural significance of TV series, but they also prove that in order to analyse seriality in a serious manner, one does not have to refer to such works as *Opałka 1965/1-∞*. It is, then, not compulsory any longer to ennoble seriality as an avant-garde means of expression in order to grasp its originality.

In other words, seriality can be analysed without leaving the field where it is most significant today and from where it seems to be propagating to other spheres of culture. It may be, then, approached as a basic characteristic of TV series that defines their aesthetic qualities. Such analyses are offered, among others, by a number of scholars who have adopted and adapted instruments of narratology and who concentrate on narrative structures and mechanisms organizing stories in TV series.[19] These aspects may be, however, approached from yet another point of view, namely that of philosophical aesthetics which may show how seriality determines the ontology of TV series as well as their reception.

2.4 *The Meaning of Seriality*

Given that the idea of seriality is not univocal, it will be useful to define what we mean by seriality.[20] The idea of seriality and its significance for the audiovisual form that we are investigating will be consistently introduced and developed below, especially in the passages where the relationships *between* episodes of TV series will be discussed. Let us, however, anticipate our arguments and present right away some intuitions concerning seriality following in the footsteps of Christy Mag Uidhir (2013).

At the outset it should be noticed that there is a dichotomy in the art world (and outside of it) between single objects that are artworks and "sets" of objects that are also works of art. Botticelli's *Primavera* is an example of the former group, whereas Władysław Strzeminski's *Unistic compositions* or the parts of *Matrix* are examples of the latter. Strzeminski's paintings, as well as the

---

19 See e.g. "Cahier de narratologie" (2016).

20 Seriality is understood in a variety of ways, which results in different typologies of serial phenomena. Apart from the books quoted above see also e.g. Cardini (2014), D'Alessandro (1984), Eco (1985), Garcìa (2016).

parts of Wachowskis' trilogy, are clearly "linked" to each other in a certain way, contrary to the Renaissance painting which is a stand-alone work.

Let us now assume for the sake of argument that a sequence is a linear concatenation of elements, whereas a series is a sum of those elements. Below, we will focus on works that consist of "linked" elements in a way that these element form not only sequences but also series. TV series are such works.

Works of art may be linked together in two distinct ways, a trivial one and non-trivial one (ibid.: 262). The trivial way of linking them consists of creating sequences that are meant to "tell" a narrative. Such a sequence may be made of e.g. St. Mark's basilica in Venice, Malevich's *Black Square* and Chopin's *Mazurek in D major*. What such a sequence may tell us has nothing to do with the philosophical or aesthetic impact of its elements (it tells us nothing about their nature, history, or preferable manner of experiencing them). In other words, a trivial sequence may be an unrestricted juxtaposition of elements made at one's will, whereas a non-trivial sequence is one in which the elements have a position defined by their relations to other elements as well as to the whole, just as it is the case with Opałka's work.

There is yet another version of trivial seriality regarding single artworks. Consider Susanna Clarke's outstanding fantasy novel *Jonathan Strange & Mr Norrell*. This is a very long and complex narrative that for the sake of clarity (as *many* other novels) is divided into chapters (in this case: twenty-five). Naturally, we can speak of seriality in this case as its chapters form a sequence which we follow while reading the book and moving from one chapter to the another. However, such seriality does not significantly influence our aesthetic experience of *Jonathan Strange & Mr Norrell*, since we still read it as a singular and wholly unified yet chaptered work. The "elements" of that novel (chapters) are made solely for the reader's convenience.

These two faces of the trivial sort of seriality are beyond the scope of our argument as we will focus on non-trivial seriality. Non-trivial seriality implies that the manner in which works are linked to each other within a series is significant for the form of art to which all the single elements of the series (the work) belong to. We thus claim that an *X* is a serial work of art if and only if it consists of elements (x1, x2, x3...) joined together in a non-trivial way and that an adequate (or most rewarding) experience and understanding of *X* is only possible through experiencing and understanding its single elements (x1, x2, x3....) in the order prescribed by *X* (Ibid.).[21]

21 While we quote the definition of serial art offered by Christy Mag Uidhir, we purposefully overlook his further analyses of what he calls, "homogenously serial art: in which every element of *X* is treated as a separate work of art. In so far as we are not concerned with

In other words, we understand seriality as non-trivial, i.e. we claim that the sequence of episodes of a TV series is a factor which is philosophically and aesthetically important in so far as their ontology, *diegesis*, and reception are concerned. Later on, we will introduce and justify the distinction between TV series strictly speaking and TV serials. Here we would just like to sketch this issue by saying that TV series as a module of storytelling consist of episodes that are *not* necessary connected, whereas TV serials always consist of a sequence of connected episodes. That is, the action contained in the episodes is continued and developed in other episodes. In this study, however, we deal with productions that are a sort of narrative hybrid—productions which have qualities typical for trivially serial works, but which are nevertheless non-trivially serial.[22] Unless specified otherwise, when we use the term "TV series" we mean both strict TV series and TV serials.

We are aware of the fact that TV series are created, distributed, and consumed in various contexts, yet we think that—as the quotation in the introduction states—seriality, conceived of in the way explained above, is a constant feature of every TV series no matter when and where it was created or watched. This is the reason why we associate seriality with normativity that is ontological as well as aesthetic.

We claim that seriality defines the ontological structure of TV series. Its presence or absence in a TV show determines whether it is a TV series or not. Seriality may assume different forms for many reasons, even the most pragmatic ones, but generally speaking seriality itself has to remain untouched. Given that seriality may be (and in fact is) shaped in various manners, there may be (and are) many TV series expressing them and hence it is possible to make their different typologies.

Seriality is also aesthetically significant because it has to be recognized by the viewers, otherwise they will not experience (appreciate) a TV series as a TV series. Failing to realise that content is structured by non-trivial seriality will, in all likelihood, lessen the aesthetic satisfaction achieved.

3 Authority, Norms, and Categories

It is quite hard to deny that beauty is an exceptionally desired aesthetic property. To say that "*A* is *B*", where *A* is an object and *B* is the property of being

deciding whether TV series are works of art, we do not need to ruminate on the artistic status of individual episodes" (2013: 263).

22 This issue is analysed in section 5.

beautiful, is to judge that *A* is valuable. For both theoretical and practical reasons, it is crucial to have the power to judge whether a given object—under specific circumstances or otherwise—is beautiful or not. The universality of judgments of beauty, labelled by Immanuel Kant as judgments of taste, is rooted in their normativity. According to Kant:

> when [a man] puts a thing on a pedestal and calls it beautiful, he demands the same delight from others. He judges not merely for himself, but for all men, and then speaks of beauty as if it were a property of things. Thus he says that the *thing* is beautiful; and it is not as if he counts on others agreeing with him in his judgment of liking owing to his having found them in such agreement on a number of occasions, but he *demands* this agreement of them. He blames them if they judge differently, and denies them taste, which he still requires of them as something they ought to have; and to this extent it is not open to men to say: Everyone has his own taste. This would be equivalent to saying that there is no such thing as taste, i.e. no aesthetic judgment capable of making a rightful claim upon the assent of all men.
>
> KANT 1790: 52

Judgments of taste are universal which means that they obtain for everyone and that they are the subject of the substantial (not merely verbal) disagreements.[23] In other words, judgments of taste are not arbitrary and express a normative attitude. Such normativity stems from the following two facts: (1) some judgments are *correct*, whereas others are *incorrect* and (2) some judgments are *better* than others (Zangwill 2003/2014: §1.2, Andina 2017b: 152). If that is so, then, these facts seem to have far-reaching and non-trivial consequences. Firstly, the moment of forming a judgement of taste is governed by the following *rule*: when person *O* under circumstances *p*[24] perceives an object *A*, then *O* should formulate the judgment: "*A* is *B*". A person who does not fulfil this obligation is vulnerable to criticism (as Kant himself points out in the cited passage).[25] Secondly, we may ask whether there is a *law* that forces

23 Such kinds of disagreements are crucial for both science and philosophy. Cf. Chalmers (2011).

24 Following the aesthetic tradition, we may say that an aesthetic judgment over *A* is only possible when we have direct contact with *A*. See Budd (2003).

25 The critical dimension of philosophical aesthetics seems to still be very valuable. Nowadays, such discussion is present among the proponents of so-called everyday aesthetics. This subfield of aesthetics should be as critical as art-centred aesthetics is. See e.g. Dowling (2010), Ratiu (2013).

us to judge: "*A* is *B*". Without any doubt, this is quite a controversial issue since it seems intuitive to say that aesthetic judgments are normative in nature, but at the same time—also guided by common intuitions—it is hard to say that it is possible to formulate any laws of the form: "For all S (S being a qualified subject) any *x* (where *x* is a work of art, a poem, sonata, etc.) that has the property X will be *pro tanto* a cause of the [aesthetic] pleasure to S" (Mothersill 1984: 101). Agreeing with the later, we might rightly ask if there are some *norms* that help us to formulate aesthetic judgments and ontological-artistic judgments.[26] If there are any such norms then we should recognize *who* is the source of such a set of norms. Clearly, in a number of fields (as in law and ethics to name just a few) there are institutions that are responsible for establishing, introducing, and protecting norms.[27] Such institutions are authorities.[28]

Józef Bocheński argues that if someone is called an authority by some other person, it implies the following relation: (x, y, α), where x is an authority for y; y is the person for whom x is the authority, and α is a field or domain of authority (see Brożek 2013a: 116). Bocheński defines authority in the following manner:

> The field of authority is a class of objectively meaningful utterances. By this is meant that it must be a class of utterances, that is, of symbols perceivable by the subject, of meaningful symbols, such as may be understood by him, and finally, that it must carry some objective meaning. Only objectively meaningful utterances may be accepted by the subject, and the acceptance of them seems to be essential to the authority [...]
>
> There are two main classes of utterances carrying complete objective meaning, namely, sentences and imperatives. Accordingly, there are two main ways of accepting an utterance: a sentence will be accepted as true, or at least as possessing a certain probability, an imperative as binding. And if so, we have to deal with two quite different sorts of authority, according to the nature of their fields: the first one, that of uttering

26 Tiziana Andina rightly points out that when we face contemporary art the most basic judgment formulated about works of art is ontological-artistic judgment—the judgment that determines the ontological status of the work of art as experienced by us. See Andina (2017a, 2017b, 2017c).

27 For the sake of the argument provided in this study, it is not necessary to wholly determine the nature of norms as such. See Haack (2005), Marmor (2011), Brożek (2013b).

28 In law and social sciences there are a number of conceptualizations regarding the distinction between authorities: cognitive authority vs. administrative authority (Walton 1997), epistemic authority and executive authority (De George 1985), and authority over belief vs. authority over conduct (Lukes 1978). The first authority is a source of knowledge, and the second one is responsible for establishing norms that must be followed.

> sentences, will be called here “epistemic authority”; the second, uttering imperatives, “deontic authority”.
>
> BOCHEŃSKI 1965: 164

The relationship between the two authorities is described by Bocheński as follows:

> Let us take the case of a lieutenant who is highly skilled in military science, and who is under the command of a rather unintelligent and uninstructed major [...]. This major is, for our lieutenant, a deontic authority in the field of imperatives concerning war actions. He can command him for example to undertake an action Q, and the lieutenant has to accept this command as binding. But in our case the lieutenant is not bound to accept any sentence, not even the sentence corresponding to the command received: “The imperative prescribing Q is tactically justified”. For only an epistemic authority can prescribe a sentence, not a deontic one. In other words, the epistemic authority is that of an expert, the deontic authority that of a commander or superior. [...] It is not implied that epistemic and deontic authority always occur in separate and distinct persons. On the contrary, the normal case, for example, in the army, will be that the same person is at the same time an expert and a commander. But it does not need to be so.
>
> BOCHEŃSKI 1965: 167–168

Our lives are full of different authorities: experts in exotic or domestic fields, or ordinary persons that are responsible for creating and introducing norms that we—as individuals subjected to these authorities—must follow.[29] Following the deontic authority allows us to make some predictions regarding our social, political, and economic life: if someone respects authority (e.g. government), then she or he is going to obey the authority’s will. For example, when an authority demands following an order (“Attack the castle!”) that we refuse to undertake, then disobeying such authority results in the non-existence of certain states of affairs. In such a case we may face a number of legally defined sanctions (e.g. be imprisoned). Law is a domain where

29 Melisa Stevanovic interestingly states that: “Epistemic authority is about getting the ‘words to match the world;’ deontic authority is about getting the ‘world to match the words.’ While epistemic authority is about knowing what is true, deontic authority is about determining what ‘ought—to-be’—what will be forbidden, obligatory, or permissible (the ancient Greek word *deon*, ‘that which is binding’)” (2013: 19).

we clearly meet these two types of authorities. The deontic authority is the legislator, whereas the epistemic authority is e.g. a respected scholar in law. These two authorities might—quite rarely though—be shared by the same individual: when the legislator is an expert in law. Interestingly, what philosophical aesthetics does not share with law is deontic authority. This is because in aesthetics it is not possible to find individuals that are able to formulate laws like "every *A* is *B*".[30] However, in philosophical aesthetics epistemic authorities may be easily found. This role is reserved for art experts or critics (see Lopes 2015). Moreover, the lack of deontic authority in aesthetics does not mean that there are no *norms* that allow people to *correctly* experience and understand works of art. Not following such norms is free of any sanctions but—at the same time—doing so prevents (or, at least obstructs) one from understanding and experiencing artworks. Let us focus on this issue in more detail.

The possibility of normative appreciation of works of art is mostly emphasized in Kendall Walton's seminal and widely cited article "Categories of Art" (1970).[31] It was a polemic against wide spread (at that time) formalism in the theory of art and aesthetics. Formalism says, roughly, that aesthetic appreciation is grounded only in intrinsic properties of the works of art (e.g. Beardsley 1958, Bell 1914). In other words, facts about the emotional state of the artist or her political or religious beliefs should not (and—in fact—do not) have any fundamental relevance for aesthetic appreciation of the work of art. Walton disagrees and argues in favour of the claim that in some (perhaps even in all) cases non-aesthetic facts, e.g. the context of an artwork's creation, are of crucial importance not only for the aesthetic experience of the artwork but mostly for the possibility of understanding the artwork. Acknowledging the non-aesthetic facts concerning an artwork allows us to formulate correct (aesthetic) judgments about it.

Walton states that the aesthetic properties of a particular work of art depend on seeing that artwork within perceptually distinguishable categories of art. By "category" he understands media, forms, styles and genres. For example, as a category of art we might distinguish gothic painting, early renaissance architecture, neoplasticism, or kinetic sculpture, etc. Moreover, under the label "perceptually distinguishable" we should understand the fact that what decides

30 Except perhaps some dictatorships but then we would rather face a legal law rather than an aesthetic one.

31 For those familiar with Walton's paper it is clear enough that the text in itself consists of a large number of well-chosen comments and thought-provoking examples. For the sake of simplicity, we focus only on theses that are directly relevant for this study. In preparing this part of the following overview, we found Brian Laetz's critical and clear commentary on Walton's seminal paper exceptionally helpful. See Laetz (2010).

whether a given object belongs to a particular category of art depends on perceptual properties. Aesthetic properties exemplified by artworks are grounded not only in non-aesthetic properties (upon which they supervene)[32] but also identifying whether these properties are "standard", "variable", and "contra-standard" for us *with regard to* a given category of art. Standard properties are those in virtue of which artworks belong to a category of art. A lack of standard properties automatically excludes the artwork from belonging to a particular category of art. Variable properties remain "neutral" in terms of belonging to a category of art. That is, if a property *B* is variable within the category *Y* the fact that the artwork *X* has *B* or not is irrelevant for *X* belonging to *Y*. The opposite story can be told for contra-standard properties. Possessing these properties automatically excludes an artwork from a particular category of art. Walton explains the relationship between standard, variable, and contra-standard properties in the following way:

> The flatness of a painting and the motionlessness of its markings are standard, and its particular shapes and colors are variable, relative to the category of painting. A protruding three-dimensional object or an electrically driven twitching of the canvas would be contra-standard relative to this category. The straight lines in stick figure drawings and squarish shapes in cubist paintings are standard with respect to those categories respectively, though they are variable with respect to the categories of drawing and painting. The exposition-development-recapitulation form of a classical sonata is standard, and its thematic material is variable, relative to the category of sonatas.
>
> WALTON 1970: 540

A single artwork can be understood and experienced as belonging to a number of different art categories. For example, *Primavera* stored at the Uffizi Gallery in Florence is seen as a painting, a renaissance piece, and an object of Sandro Botticelli's style.[33] The circumstances under which we familiarize ourselves with an artwork may have an influence on our perception and understanding of the categories of art it belongs to (1970: 341–342). Firstly, it is important to consider what categories of art we know before encountering the work itself. Being familiar with a particular category of art maximalizes the chance

32 Walton explicitly follows Frank Sibley's considerations here regarding the relationship between aesthetic and non-aesthetic properties (of artworks). See Sibley (1965).

33 The work was, of course, created by Botticelli. However, to enter the category of "being Botticelli-style" it is not necessary for a given work to have been created by Botticelli.

of understanding the encountered artwork within that particular category. Secondly, professional expertise and the opinions of the others have a huge impact on an individual's ability to recognize a given category of art. According to Walton, this is especially noticeable when we face a category pertaining to the artistic style of an individual artist—without guidance from friends or teachers/art lovers it might be quite difficult to recognize the style of the same artist across a few artworks. Lastly, the way in which we get acquainted with a work of art has a certain significance for recognizing its correct category. For example, when admiring Joseph Kosuth's *One and Three Chairs* at a contemporary art exhibition, it is much easier to qualify and experience/understand it as conceptual art than when coming across it at an American art (broadly construed) exhibition.

The concept of art categories as well as the understanding of standard, variable, and contra-standard properties of artworks as determined by particular categories have a direct influence on the human experience of artworks and art in general. This is emphatically shown in Walton's example on Pablo Picasso's *Guernica*:

> Imagine a society which does not have an established medium of painting, but does produce a kind of work of art called *guernicas*. *Guernicas* are like versions of Picasso's "Guernica" done in various bas-relief dimensions. All of them are surfaces with the colors and shapes of Picasso's "Guernica," but the surfaces are molded to protrude from the wall like relief maps of different kinds of terrain. Some *guernicas* have rolling surfaces, others are sharp and jagged, still others contain several relatively flat planes at various angles to each other, and so forth. Picasso's "Guernica" would be counted as a *guernica* in this society—a perfectly flat one—rather than as a painting. Its flatness is variable and the figures on its surface are standard relative to the category of *guernicas*. Thus the flatness, which is standard for us, would be variable for members of the other society (if they should come across "Guernica") and the figures on the surface, which are variable for us, would be standard for them. This would make for a profound difference between our aesthetic reaction to "Guernica" and theirs. It seems violent, dynamic, vital, disturbing to us. But I imagine it would strike them as cold, stark, lifeless, or serene and restful or perhaps bland, dull, boring—but in any case not violent, dynamic, and vital. We do not pay attention to or take note of "Guernica" 's flatness; this is a feature we take for granted in paintings, as it were. But for the other society this is "Guernica" 's most striking and noteworthy characteristic—what is *expressive* about it. Conversely, "Guernica" 's

> color patches, which we find noteworthy and expressive, are insignificant to them.
>
> WALTON 1970: 347

Whether a single property, e.g. flatness, is standard, variable, or contra-standard depends on what category of art the work belongs to. In the case of the Picasso's masterpiece flatness is a standard property, whereas in the case of a *guernica* flatness is variable property in virtue of (a hypothetical) category of art. In that example, the flatness of a *guernica* seems to be a more profound factor for our aesthetic experience than in the case of *Guernica.* The scenario brings forth the issue of perceiving the categories of art as well. In other words, what category is proper/correct for a particular artwork? Can we even deliberate on any kind of "correctness"? As has been noted, every work of art might be seen as belonging to different categories of art. This is obviously true, and such a number of possibilities has undeniable aesthetic potential. For example, *Guernica* as a painting is vivid and brutal but as a *guernica* it appears to be dull and unoriginal. A simple answer to the question formulated above is to say that our aesthetic judgments are category-relative. An object *x* has a property *C* under the description *Y*, whereas *x* has a property *B* under the description *X*. Again, *Guernica* is vivid and brutal as a painting and dull and unoriginal as a *guernica.* The obvious advantage of such an answer is to admit that both aesthetic judgements are mutually compatible since they refer to the same object experienced under very different (and incompatible) categories of art, where categories are responsible for fixing a set of properties that are standard, variable, and contra-standard. This has a direct consequence for aesthetic experience and appreciation.

Clearly enough, Walton rejects this interpretation of the nature of aesthetic judgements. He refuses to admit that our aesthetic judgements are category-relative (1970: 355–357).[34] The reason that motivates his sentiment is simply admitting that if this is true, then our aesthetic judgments differ from each other in too narrowly. The argument in favour of refusing the category-relativeness of judgments is designed to keep and protect the critical dimension of philosophy of art and aesthetics in general. (Assuming that in aesthetics we have substantial and not just merely verbal disputes and disagreements). It is in fact true that when we are admiring a work of conceptual art as belonging

34 Walton sees room for such category-relative aesthetics judgements in nature. This becomes a very powerful idea within the aesthetics of nature and might be treated as root of cognitivism regarding aesthetic experience of nature. See e.g. Carlson (1981, 1999), Parsons (2002, 2006).

to the category of classical sculpture or as representational art we make *a mistake*. In addition, when the mistake is noticed we are willing to revise our previous attitude (e.g. when a good friend explained us *what* object we encountered) and admit that our earlier categorization was simply wrong. Walton says:

> Thus it seems that, at least in some cases, it is correct to perceive a work in certain categories, and incorrect to perceive it in certain others; that is, our judgments of it when we perceive it in the former are likely to be true, and those we make when perceiving it in the latter false. This provides us with absolute senses of "standard," "variable," and "contra-standard": features of a work are standard, variable, or contra-standard absolutely just in case they are standard, variable, or contra-standard (respectively) for people who perceive the work correctly.
>
> WALTON 1970: 356–357

The cited passage is of crucial importance here. Walton claims not only that some categories and judgments based on them are incorrect, whereas other categories and judgments are correct. He also claims that properties (standard, variable, and contra-standard) are absolute and, thus, are not subject to change for those individuals that perceive the work of art *correctly*. Walton suggests four rules or criteria that might help us in recognizing which category of art is correct for a given work of art (1970: 357–358). For a work of art *X* and the category *Y* it is important that: (1) *X* consists of a maximally big number of standard properties for *Y* and a minimal number (preferably: none) of contra-standard properties for *Y*; (2) *X* is perceived as belonging to *Y* which brings an interesting interpretation of *X*, and *X* possess a considerably high aesthetic impact—these both suggest that *Y* is a correct category for experiencing and understanding *X*; (3) if the artist created *X* with the intention of belonging to *Y*, then there is a good chance that *Y* is a correct category for *X*; and, finally, (4) at the moment when *X* is brought into existence, *Y* is an established category within the art world and most people perceive *X* as belonging to *Y*.[35]

35 The traditional interpretation of Walton's theory is to admit that by a "correct category" for a work of art *x* we should understand the categories that *x* really belongs to. That is, *guernica* is an incorrect category for *Guernica* since *Guernica* is not a *guernica*, and being a painting is correct for *Guernica* since *Guernica* is really a piece of painted art. However, an alternative theory might be provided. It says that Walton's theory is not aimed at determining the correct categories for artworks (Laetz 2010: 295). Or, at least, we should understand "correct category" in a different way. The alternative interpretation says that the correct categories for an artwork *x* are the categories that make *x* "aesthetically active"

To sum up: Walton's theory refers to the necessity of determining the correct categories to which a particular work of art belongs. Categories have a non-trivial role in realizing the aesthetic impact of artworks. Walton's view is echoed in a huge number of papers devoted to analytic aesthetics and beyond. In our opinion, the most vivid inspirations of that kind can be found in the conceptions of *generic interpretation* and *artist's sanctions upon artwork*. Let us elaborate them a bit.

The first one concerns the relationship between interpretation and the interpreted object. It is obvious that we interpret a large group of things: ancient symbols, artefacts of unknown origin, our best friend's facial expressions, or the intentions of colleague we do not like. All of these objects belong to very different ontological categories: physical objects, processes, or mental states respectively. Despite the evident differences between them, there is something that connects them all: at a certain moment these objects have (for an individual or a group of people) an ambiguous meaning which must be clarified.[36] Usually, what we interpret are cultural objects (Margolis 2010). That means, simplifying greatly, that cultural objects are intentionally created by (human) agents.[37] This issue is particularly self-evident when we admit that perceptually indistinguishable objects may have radically different meanings. Arthur C. Danto notably explained this issue in a thought experiment in which we are asked to imagine a series of perceptually identical red squares: *Kierkegaard's Mood, Red Square* (realist), *Red Square* (minimalist version), *Nirvana, Red Table Cloth*, a canvas grounded in red lead prepared by Giorgione (not an artwork), a painted surface (not an artwork), and a painting described by Kierkegaard of Israelites crossing the Red Sea (Danto 1989: 39). The listed objects consist of both non-artworks and artworks. In the latter group we have a few (incompatible) meanings—certainly, *Red Square* (realist) and *Red Square* (minimalist version) differ from each other significantly. The ability to be an interpretable object is very important if we think of the ontological status of that object. Danto, at the beginning of *The Transfiguration of the Commonplace*, states that "Indiscernible objects become quite different and distinct works of art by dint

(Ibid.). Although this is an interesting issue in and of itself, we must leave it unsolved here.

36 There is no need to assume that the process of interpretation must last forever. Usually, once we clarify the meaning the process stops. Of course, one might think of exceptions where interpretations go on endlessly. Such exceptions are often works of art.

37 Of course, interpretation of cultural objects goes beyond identifying the intentions of their creators. This is, however, often crucial because the intention allows us (at least, partly) to determine the object's properties.

of distinct and different interpretations, so I shall think of interpretations as functions which transform material objects into works of art" (1989: 1ff).

Leaving aside the problem of whether interpretation in fact possess transformative power (in the ontological sense) with regard to "mere objects" which are turned into works of art, the following question might be asked: How should one interpret objects? Or, probably better: what is the *necessary* condition for being the correct interpretation of artworks? In his answer to this question, Peter Lamarque states that interpretation starts with interpreting a concrete token of artwork, e.g. a such-and-such song or a such-and-such graphic novel, belonging to artforms or art styles that are well-known to us (2010: 159). In the same place he also says that: "Interpretation gets under away, indeed made possible, in the light of prior knowledge about what kind of thing, broadly conceived, the object of interpretation is. The enabling assumption is that the work under investigation belongs in a recognizable generic category" (2010: 159–160). The kind of interpretation that enables recognition of an ontological category of an artwork is *generic interpretation* (2010: 162). It is an indispensable element of meaning-determining interpretation, which is simply determination of the content of the artwork. Here we might notice an explicit reference to Walton's theory. Lamarque goes even further since for him determining the correct category is essential for perceiving artworks' meaning, whereas Walton is mainly concerned about the aesthetic impact of artworks.

Artists create artworks and give us a plethora of interesting interpretations of them. But they also put special kinds of *sanctions* upon artworks. In Sherri Irvin's opinion, sanctions are especially important in contemporary art where we experience a huge number of works that undergo constant alterations over time. Nowadays we are surrounded by a constantly growing number of artworks that have no "fixed" properties throughout their persistence. To know what properties an artwork has, we must first establish its spatial boundaries. That is, where it starts and where it ends.[38] What helps are sanctions that are put in place by the artist upon the artwork, i.e. public actions and statements that illuminate the nature of the art work. Sherri Irvin understands sanctions as follows:

> The most common way for an artist to sanction particular features of his or her work is by presenting an object within a particular context [...] In addition, some features of the artwork are fixed by actions and

38 This is a key issue for correct interpretations of artworks. In interpretation, an individual implicitly assumes that the work of art is grasped as a whole and not as a part of something.

> communications other than the creation or presentation of the art object. Through these actions and communications, such as giving the work a title, offering an artist statement to accompany the work, or instructing curators about conservation or the conditions of display, the artist establishes a sanction of certain features of the work.
>
> IRVIN 2005: 229–230

The role of sanctions is not to provide the privileged interpretation of the work but to define the very nature of the work of art. Thus, sanctions play an ontological role. For example, if an artwork is made from very impermanent medium, say, sugar, then the role of the artist is to establish whether the destroyed parts of the work (e.g. in a sculpture) might be replaced with new elements or not. Sanctions appear to be certain parameters determining the existence and properties of artworks. Discovering artists' sanctions is crucial with contemporary art which often breaks, redefines, and revises the well-known criteria and rules that governs traditional artistic production. Again, the reference to Walton's theory is pretty straightforward. To put it simply: when experiencing artworks, we must know what they are and how we should approach them.

The above considerations allow us to think that we actually have norms in philosophical aesthetics. These norms aim at enabling the individual to understand and experience an artwork correctly. We propose to enumerate two such norms. They are not nomological in nature (so, they can be broken) but rather rules promoting valuable contact with artworks. For an artwork x: (1) *The Categorial Norm*: is to discover x's categories, ontological nature, and the sanctions put upon it, and (2) *The Aesthetic Norm*: is to maximalize the aesthetic impact of x. There is a hierarchy between the norms; the first refers to ontological-artistic judgments on artworks, whereas the second refers to aesthetic judgements. It seems that *The Categorial Norm* is more important because following *The Aesthetic Norm* depends on how we fulfil the categorial one.[39]

In this section the role of authority and normativity in philosophical aesthetics has been presented and discussed. We sketched the idea that correct interpretation and understanding of art objects is always connected with some sort of normativity. That is, some aesthetic judgments are correct, whereas others are incorrect, and some correct aesthetics judgments are better than the others. It is suggested as well that although there are no laws—strictly

39 It is worth noting that these norms seem to be neutral with regard to particular definitions of art. The necessary and sufficient conditions for being an artwork within a given definition of art are independent from The Categorial Norm and The Aesthetic Norm.

speaking—in the field of philosophical aesthetics, we may still reasonably think of norms that guide our aesthetic experience and encounters with the arts. The norms refer to the need for determining the real ontological nature of the art object and to the maximalisation of its aesthetic impact. Normativity in the arts is manifested in the specific hierarchy that can be reduced to the motto: ontology goes before aesthetics. In the next sections, we shall propose a model for understanding the role of norms in the ontology and aesthetics of television narratives. We argue that not following *The Categorial Norm* and *The Aesthetic Norm* when watching and thinking of TV series may have a non-trivial influence on our experience, viewing practices, and understanding of this form of popular art.

4 Qualities and Complexities of Television

4.1 *Television Aesthetics*

Contemporary TV series are interesting cultural phenomena not only for the reasons discussed by media theory and cultural studies, but also from an aesthetic point of view which, in fact, is sometimes tentatively taken into account by series studies scholars. Yet, the philosophical approach we are going to suggest is different.

If TV series are discussed in in terms of aesthetics, the debates tend to follow the general agenda of television aesthetics. They are usually aimed at deciding whether TV series may be considered art or not and whether it is possible to establish criteria indispensable for analysing their qualities.[40] The latter issue also seems to largely determine the way media theory or cultural studies understand aesthetics, i.e. as criticism, which immediately makes everyone suspicious of it as it inevitably appears to be a tool of ideological power.

Aesthetics as criticism is often associated with aesthetics as discourse on narrative.[41] Aesthetics is therefore taken to mean either aesthetic qualities of the content of TV series or the way the content is conveyed. In a word, aesthetics, seen by media theory and cultural studies as a factor that shapes narratives and is shaped by them, tends to be understood in a very general and

40 The current debates on television aesthetics, including discussions of TV series, are summarized in e.g. Cardwell (2013), Nannicelli (2016), Zborowski (2016).

41 For example, there is a section called "narratives/aesthetic/criticism" in the periodical "TV/Series".

heterogeneous manner and thus covers a variety of issues concerning production, distribution, and consumption of TV series.[42]

Aesthetic analyses are sometimes focused on seriality too, albeit, more often than not, they are aimed at offering various typologies of TV series based upon scrutiny of existing works. In spite of the unquestionable usefulness of such approaches, there seems to be more to be said about seriality, especially if we shift to the standpoint inherent to philosophical aesthetics. Our approach may be then related to the "aesthetic turn",[43] as we assume that "if we are interested in historical or contemporary media culture and media arts, we need to study not only the content of artefacts but also their form" (Manovich 2017: 10).

Although philosophical aesthetics may provide criticism within a theoretical framework, it decisively refrains from critical judgments. Our intention is therefore to offer a suggestion of what the foundations for an "aesthetic method of interpretation—an attentiveness to tone, to plot and character, to visual strategies, to the workings of narrative" (Thorburn 1987: 165) could be. Such foundations may be laid, among other things, by analysis of seriality which is—as has already been said—the meeting point of production, distribution, and consumption with all their contingencies discussed by series studies and yet is a constant factor that makes TV series what they are no matter how their aesthetics may appear to media theorists and cultural studies scholars.

In this sense philosophical aesthetics applied to TV series is focused on what we take to be the basic "level", which is in a sense prior to the levels discussed by other disciplines interested in seriality and television. Seriality, as we conceive it, (1) defines the ontology of TV series which in turn (2) defines their aesthetic properties as well as (3) determines the way they are watched, which we are going to call the "standard" manner. This is our triple claim, which we will endeavour to clarify while arguing that seriality implies normativity.

It may seem that questioning the aesthetic potential of the contemporary television is doomed to failure. Without a doubt, television is able to elicit valuable aesthetic experiences from viewers, and this bare fact is good enough to include the televisual medium within the purview of philosophical aesthetics.[44] Acknowledging this point does not, however, neutralize the specific difficulty in establishing the relationship between "television"

---

42 On that topic see e.g. Creeber (2013), Eichner, Mikos, and Winter (2013), Metallinos (2013), Peacock and Jacobs (2013), Thompson (2003), Ulrich and Knape (2014).

43 An interesting discussion of it may be found on the Antenna blog: http://blog.commarts.wisc.edu/category/columns/the-aesthetic-turn/ [last accessed on 03/29/18].

44 On some markers of the aesthetic and aesthetics cf. Levinson (2003).

and "aesthetics".[45] In other words, stating this fact is not enough in purely philosophical terms. In particular, the following questions remain: how is it possible for television to exemplify aesthetic properties? Does every television programme exemplify aesthetic properties? Setting these questions aside, we might fairly easily say that the experiences we get while watching television are *very* similar in nature to those encountered when we admire such artforms as sculpture, film, or music. If so, then at least some individuals may argue that television (or to be more precise: some of its instances, e.g. programmes) can be included in the artworld.[46]

Generally speaking, it is easy to see that the traditional distinction between high and low art is still widespread (Fisher 2001). The former is art that moves the human soul, exemplifies rare and profound aesthetic qualities, remains focused on the moral transformation of society; it is elitist, and it is valuable for its own sake. The latter appears to be something more common, less intellectual and less profound than high art. The difference between the two types of art is valuating in nature. That is, works of high art are often perceived as more precious than objects of low art. An interesting version of this division is the demarcation between serious art and entertainment (Shusterman 2003). Obviously, low art cannot be completely identified with entertainment since many instances of entertainment are simply not art at all. Nonetheless, this type of art shares a lot with amusement and is often created purely for our pleasure and enjoyment. Such art is less valuable and sophisticated than serious art, which is not primarily made for the sake of joy. High art may be represented by, for example, sculpture or painting whereas low art is represented by popular music or graphic novels. The above distinction can be immediately translated into television and ends up classifying television as a form of the mediocre type.

Regardless of whether the high/low art distinction is true or not,[47] it allows us to think of an interesting issue within television aesthetics that is

45 For example, Stanley Cavell (1984) explicitly notes that there is a certain tension in seeing television as a purely aesthetic object since it is quite difficult to discriminate the aesthetic possibilities of television as a medium.

46 Please note that—as we stated in the introduction—for the purpose of this study we assume that at least some television programmes, i.e. TV series, are artworks. However, many points touched on in this survey remain neutral about the artistic status of television narratives.

47 Generally speaking, contemporary scholars—for various reasons—question or even reject the distinction. As Ted Cohen provocatively noted: "If the distinction between high art and low art is like the distinction between art and non-art, then why do we need *both* distinctions? Suppose I am already lumbered with an art/non-art divide, shouldering it because I cannot seem to get along without it. Why do I also drag a wedge for separating

important for this study. Namely, *what* is the subject of the high/low distinction? Is it a distinction between: (1) forms of art, e.g. paintings versus television; (2) genres within the same artform, e.g. classic literature versus fantasy, or (3) single artworks within the same artforms, e.g. *Mickey Mouse* versus *Sandman*. (1) and (2) mean that the status of a particular artwork is determined by the form of art or artistic genre the artworks belong to. (3) refers to particular judgments about artworks, and it seems to be quite independent from artforms and genres. For example, *Anna Karenina* is an outstanding piece of romance novel and thus a token of high art, whereas a popular bodice ripper entitled *The Ultimate Betrayal* is just a token of low art. It is worth pointing out that different formats can be found within the same medium—highbrow, lowbrow, and middlebrow—and the safest option is not to judge the medium in general but rather genres and styles or even single tokens of artforms.[48]

Television aesthetics seems to understand the above discussion. It values the aesthetic experiences elicited only by some of the programmes or television formats. The purpose of television aesthetics is "a generalised understanding of the key foci of philosophical aesthetics: the criticism and evaluation of art, and the raising and tackling of questions that arise from our engagement with works of art" (Cardwell 2005: 180). In this section, we shall briefly present two dominant modules that approach the issue of the aesthetic dimension of television in slightly different ways, namely—Quality TV and Complex TV.[49]

4.2 *Quality TV*

Quality TV[50] is a style or format within contemporary television which is usually used for labelling high quality programmes that are characterised by a well-rounded visual site, non-trivial theme, significant complexity of characters, as well as mastery in creating suspense and atmosphere (cf. Caldwell 1995).[51] Examples of quality TV are marked by productions like *Twin Peaks,*

high art from low art? What extra work does it do?" (1993: 152). Emphasis in the original. See also e.g. Lavine (1988), Novitz (1992), Shusterman (1991).

48 An illuminating discussion devoted to highbrow, lowbrow, and middlebrow in culture is provided in Ryynanen (2005).

49 On new "genres" of television see also Shuster (2017).

50 The concept originated in Feurer, Keer, and Vahimagi (1984), see also McCabe and Akass (2011), Schlütz (2016).

51 An interesting definition of Quality TV is given by Robert Thompson: "Quality TV is best defined by what is not. It is not 'regular' TV". Yet, he enumerates a number of properties such as (for example): being made by artists, creating a new genre by mixing old ones, being literary and writer-based, or self-consciousness as rightly distributing Quality TV programmes (1997: 13–16). The understanding of "Quality TV" in this study is mostly fuelled by Thompson's definition.

The Sopranos, Mad Men, The Wire, Buffy the Vampire Slayer, or *Westworld*. Scholarly studies on quality TV are focused on two dominant issues. Firstly, the possibility of formulating critical judgment about quality TV programmes is examined. Where the term "quality" is understood primarily as a regulatory criterion which means that—by the definition—we are able to formulate a sort of critical judgment (Geraghty 2003: 27). Secondly, the relationship between "quality" and aesthetic properties is investigated. In particular, they examine whether every token (e.g. a programme) of quality TV is automatically good—and thus aesthetic—television or not.

Let us focus on the possibility of formulating critical judgments first. Connecting television with philosophical aesthetics naturally suggests a question regarding the normativity of aesthetic/critical judgments about programmes. In other words, are there any criteria or norms for judging whether a programme is better or worse from others? This theoretical issue has a very practical consequence: we often take for granted that good programmes deserve to be watched before (e.g. due to lack of time) or more passionately than programmes of poor quality. Jacob Jacobs rightly points out that television is not only a medium but also a way of communication (Jacobs 2000). He also says that "What distinguishes television from other media is its ability to communicate immediately in sound and image (usually, but not always, a product of its fetishized 'liveness'), and art forms are relayed, rather than produced, by television" (Jacobs 2001: 430). If we would like to make a critical judgment about a television programme or format, its specificity (as something differentiating it from other forms of art) must be taken into account. This rule applies to the medium in itself (television) as well as forms of that medium (e.g. information programmes, reality shows, soap operas, etc.). In other words, "we need to recognize that our criteria for judgement are in part derived by defining the nature of our involvement with specific texts" (ibid.).[52] An example of such a format is a TV serial. If we want to make a critical judgment of a single episode, then we should take into account the place of that episode

52 *Nb*. This issue is somehow similar to what we could come across when studying contemporary investigations on the ontological structure of art works. In order to establish the ontological category of a certain object, say, a work of art, we must also take into account our critical judgements concerning it. Amie Thomasson is quite instructive at this very point: "In order to unambiguously ground the reference of a general term to name a kind of work of art, the grounder must not only have the idea that the reference of his or her term will be an art-kind, but must also have a background conception of what *ontological* sort of art-kind he or she means the term to refer to, establishing existence conditions and identity conditions for works of that kind. Such an ontological conception then disambiguates potential reference by determining the ontological kind referred to by the art-kind term" (2005: 225). See also Davies (2004).

within the greater whole (as a season or a finished production). This is because the episode remains in a non-trivial relationship to the other episodes. This relation is both ontological and aesthetic in nature.[53]

Another topic regarding the possibility of making critical judgments—also taken from TV series—is the role of title sequences. The role matters for a whole production as well as for single episodes (cf. Gripsrud 1995). The title sequence's job is to introduce the main characters, to give the overall atmosphere flavour, and to be an interesting metacommentary for the whole plot. A good example of a title sequence and its role is *Dexter*. While watching it, we see a series of everyday domestic activities such as grinding coffee beans, brushing teeth, tying shoelaces, and putting on a T-shirt. In these apparently innocent activities, a powerful and disquieting force is hidden: the main character—Dexter Morgan—performs these activities with a certain kind of deliberation. Moreover, the dynamics of these performances unambiguously suggest brutality and murder. For example, putting on the T-shirt lasts a second too long—it imaginatively resembles suffocating someone with a pillow. Under the outwardly innocent domestic activities, a profound aggression is hidden. The title sequence highlights the main theme of the series, that is, Dexter Morgan's trials in adjusting to work and life within society. He hides his real nature as a serial killer. By applying a number of (highly sophisticated) tricks, Dexter is able to deceive other characters, but he cannot do it the viewers. When watching this TV series, the audience is aware of Dexter's murderous nature and his struggle with the urge to kill innocent people from the very beginning. He does so by ritualizing everyday activities and through ascribing them an aesthetic significance.[54] All these actions allow him to pretend that he is a regular neighbour with an uninteresting job. This is especially stressed in the last few seconds of the title sequence, when we see Dexter locking the door to his clean and neat apartment: Dexter furtively smiles to us (the viewers) since we know his deepest secret. The title sequence as described performs its role with regard to *Dexter* well as it nicely emphasises the relationship between the whole series and individual episodes (the theme of hiding the truth about Dexter Morgan's nature is crucial for the plot). Thus, *Dexter*'s title sequence gives us "the theme and tone" of the whole series (cf. Jacobs 2001: 438).

The abovementioned example invites us to think of another issue: critical judgments of television series (as a whole and as parts, i.e. episodes) are an immediate consequence of understanding what a given television format is. To

53 For more on this issue please consult sections 5.2 and 6.

54 For a detailed analysis of *Dexter*'s title sequence in terms of aesthetics, everyday performances, and violence see Golubiewski, Andrzejewski, and Kulas (2014).

frame it differently: the correct identification of the object being discussed and experienced enables a formulation of critical judgement (cf. Cardwell 2007: 20). As Charlotte Brusndon correctly points out: "the generic diversity of television must be taken into account in discussions of quality, but not in ways which make quality "genre-specific", creating certain "sink" or "trash" genres of which demands are not made" (1997: 134). The quoted passage should not be read as suggesting that "quality" is virtually independent from any television format. Such a situation is quite hard to imagine as "quality" does not refer to television as such but rather to specific programmes. However, these programmes or formats should be understood quite broadly (Geraghty 2003: 32). The intention is to keep the quality of some formats or programmes and do not give up the sort of quality of the others.

The possibility of passing critical judgments on television programmes is directly connected with the second area of interest undertaken in the scholarly study of Quality TV, namely, the relationship between "quality" and aesthetic properties. Being more precise, the following should be asked: is every programme of quality TV (e.g. a TV series) *good* television? Without a doubt, the connection between "quality TV" and "good TV" is strong, but these terms are not identical. The former is based on the possibility of identifying some textual qualities in the television programme rather than on an immediate, emotional and purely subjective reaction to the programme. The latter is coined as a label describing the overall audience's experience of the programme. As Sarah Cardwell says: "Good television is rich, riveting, moving, provocative and frequently contemporary (in some sense); it is relevant to and valued by us. It speaks to us, and it endures for us" (2007: 21). The conceptual discrepancy between these two terms implies that it is rational to say that programme *x* is well-done and exemplifies the desired textual properties—thus, classifying *x* as quality TV—and at the same time claim that we do not like *x*.

It is clear that what is and is not quality TV depends primarily on social consent. In other words, there is a critical community that (somehow) decides what programme is "serious" enough to be quality TV and what programme fails this "seriousness" (ibid.: 23). This connects with what we indicated earlier about epistemic and deontic authority.[55] The role of the epistemic authority is to point out good TV, whereas the deontic authority (as the critical community) would be determining what is or is not quality TV. A commentary is required here. First, as we pointed out in an earlier section, it is hard to say there are laws in philosophical aesthetics that are analogous to those that are widely present in the legal field. If so, then we face the very

55 See section 3.

interesting fact that the critical community is not coherent in its decisions and that various members of that community may (and actually do) classify tokens of quality TV in different ways. An example of such incoherence can be observed in studies on quality TV undertaken from national perspectives, e.g. USA (cf. McCabe and Akass 2007). Different criteria for being quality TV are formulated in the United States of America, the United Kingdom, and continental Europe. Second, the deontic authority has no power to determine what is good television. If such attempts were to be made, then we would probably be facing a form of censorship.

Indicators of quality television cannot be automatically translated into the value of the programme. However, such indicators help to make the programme better and possibly improve the overall audience's experience of it (Caldwell, 30–31). Various technical operations foster the complexity of television programmes which in turn makes them less trivial and (more) subject to interesting critical interpretations. The mutual relationship between quality TV and good TV is described by Caldwell as follows:

> To determine quality one need only refer to details of the programme and show that they exhibit fundamental defining features. To determine real value—to make a critical judgement and try to persuade others of it—one must both interpret the programme and evaluate it according to explicit criteria. 'Quality' is not synonymous with value or how good something is; it is closer to being a set of generic traits that distinguishes a group identity.
>
> CALDWELL 2007: 32

So, defining whether a given programme is quality TV or not is simply fulfilling the categorial norm—we identify the cultural object that we experience and determine the nature of that object. Whereas, making critical judgments concerning the programme (which is nothing more than another way of saying "aesthetic judgment") is fulfilling the aesthetic norm. It is worth noting that in discussions over quality TV it is important to remember about the hierarchy between norms. Determining what is "quality television" is a form of ontological-artistic judgment. It is clear that, however, this judgment automatically influences a whole set possible aesthetic judgments. For example, the TV serial *A* exemplifying a set of properties $\{x, y, z\}$ that is not quality TV may be considered valuable and good, whereas another TV serial, let's say *B*, that *is* quality TV exemplifying the same set of properties $\{x, y, z\}$ might be judged as unoriginal and dull. All this may happen since the term "quality" is not a direct indicator of artistic and aesthetic value, yet at the same time it indicates certain *expectations* about the productions that are labelled by this term.

4.3 *Complex TV*

The term "complex TV" was coined by Jason Mittell for describing a phenomenon within contemporary television. In short, the term refers to a recently emerged model of storytelling that is different from TV series or episodic-oriented narration (cf. 2006, 2013, 2014, 2015). In Mittell's project, such narrative complexity "is predicted on specific facets of storytelling that seem uniquely suited to the television series structure apart from film and literature and that distinguish it from conventional modes of episodic and serial form" (2015: 18). Complex TV is then limited not to television itself but specifically to television narratives (TV series/serials). Of course, seriality as a cultural phenomenon is well-known in the arts,[56] but the novelty of complex TV is based on the idea that it "redefines episodic forms under the influence of serial narration" (ibid.: 18). The specificity of this module is manifested in a high degree by viewers' commitment, active fandom, transmedia storytelling, and deep reception.

At first glance the above characteristics may suggests that complex TV is a genre of quality TV. Such an impression is reinforced when we realize that complex TV also confronts the question of the possibility of formulating critical judgements on television programmes, in particular, television narratives. Moreover, both quality TV and complex TV put forward the same questions: How does the audience decide which TV series is better, or is there any criteria that shapes critical judgments? Despite these convergences, complex TV and quality TV are distinct phenomena (ibid.: 216).The latter often uses a rather unclear sense of the term "quality" which simply divides existing series into two groups: ones that refer to this term, and ones that do not. A far more interesting way of probing this term is to investigate it as a label that is widely used by fan communities rather than as a concept of real critical and evaluative substance as it is often presented in academic discourse. Mittell explicitly recalls Cardwell here since she tends to understand quality TV as a style or genre and not as a direct indicator of any value. However, Mittell points out that, in Cardwell's opinion, properties that make a programme quality TV also make it better (ibid.: 212). What is more, whereas quality TV is concentrated on content, visual attractiveness, and coherence of television narratives, complex TV is more concerned with narrative and temporal relations between episodes and seasons.[57]

---

56 See section 1.

57 It is worth noting that both quality TV and complex TV tend to classify similar television series. For example, no-one denies that *Mad Men, The Sopranos*, or *The Wire* are—depending on the definition we would like to follow—epitomes of quality TV or complex TV. This does not automatically mean that these two concepts are identical. Rather, it suggests that they share *the* same object of inquiry.

When referring to the possibility of critical judgement on television narratives, he distinguishes two terms: *valuation* and *evaluation*. The first term is used as a descriptor of the judgment of to what extent a given programme (e.g. a television series) is worth our attention thanks to intrinsic properties it has. That is, how the programme is presented to us as viewers (in terms of inner authenticity, truth, etc.). The second term refers to the active engagement of the viewers in evaluating a programme's aesthetics, its perceptual qualities, or the way it exists in culture (see ibid.: 215–216). Complex TV is not quality TV also because it emphasizes the process of valuation. When judging a television work, we must take into account how this work realizes its own intrinsic assumptions or its coherence (ibid.: 218–222).

Complex TV as a module of storytelling aims at the specific kind of aesthetics Mittell calls "operational aesthetics" (ibid.: 41–54). This aesthetics goes beyond mere appreciation of formal properties exemplified by television narratives. It focuses instead on the level of self-awareness of the television work. While watching an episode we stop asking: "what would happen?" and move to more intriguing question such as "how did he do that?" In other words, the centre of aesthetic pleasure that is derived from watching a TV series is moved from the interest of knowing the plot to getting familiar with the intentions, motivations, and actions of the characters. Operational aesthetics focuses on spectacular plot twists, complexity, and narrative intensity. "Its power stems from the program's manipulation of its own *intrinsic norms*, or the patterns and expectations that a given series established for itself" (ibid.: 44).

Appreciation of a television serial depends on how the series realized its own aesthetic ambitions. It may happen that a visually outstanding production fails since it is not able to continue performing the aesthetic and narrative rhythm imposed on itself. A good example of such a television serial is *Hannibal*. All three seasons represent a high level of visual aesthetics, attention to details, spectacular costumes and choreography, as well as a huge number of atmospheric scenes presenting cooking and eating. If we want to apply the criteria derived from operational aesthetics, we might (sadly) conclude that only the first two seasons maintain a decent level of self-awareness, whereas the last does not perform the task so well. The two seasons are devoted to Dr. Hannibal Lecter's murders, his complicated and passionate relations with Will Graham and Jack Crawford, as well as endeavours to catch Dr. Lecter. The last season tells the story of Lecter's European trip and developing queer relationship with Graham. Through the two first seasons we might admire complex intrigue and plotting by Dr. Lecter, but in the last season—when almost all the cards were on the table—the viewers witness a record of the main characters' inner emotions and quandaries. This might be enjoyable, but it rather fails to create a successful crime fiction or thriller.[58]

5 Everything Is Connected: The Relations between Episodes

In the previous sections we have shown how the phenomenon of seriality is connected with television aesthetics. Seriality is defined as a module that fragmentizes the plot and brings a sense of order to the parts of television works. The role of the categorial and aesthetic norms has been elaborated as well.[59] That is, the importance of determining the real ontological status of the work and linking it with the maximalisation of its aesthetic potential has been spelled out. The following part of the survey is devoted to the ontology of television series. In other words, what is given when we follow the categorial norm. Our purpose is to show and elaborate the necessary conditions of television serial narratives. These conditions describing the categorial nature of television narratives are crucial for determining viewers' aesthetic appreciation of TV series. We propose to enumerate two such conditions: (1) the *quasi*-causal relations between episodes and (2) the temporal relations between episodes.

5.1 *Modes of TV Drama Narrations: Series, Non-continuous Serials, and Continuous Serials*

Several types of television narration can be listed (see e.g. Carocci 2004, Fulton, Huisman, Murphet, and Dunn 2005, Allrath and Gymnich 2005, Berger 1997). We would like to focus exclusively on the one narrative distinction that has importance for the purpose of this study, that is, the series/serial distinction (cf. Fiske 1987: 150, Oltean 1993: 13, Mittell 2015: 235).

Television series is a mode of storytelling that consists of single episodes. These episodes might be narratively connected (in terms of plot), but usually episodes have different storylines. In other words, each episode has a self-contained plot. This type of storytelling is sometimes referred to as episodic narrative (cf. Mittell 2015: 19–20, 22–23). When we think of series—frankly speaking—we have an number of episodes and seasons in mind. The initial

58 This task is, however, nicely performed in *Mindhunters*.

59 Moreover, it is instructive to think of normativity within the narrative arts (as e.g. television dramas or films) as something regarding the form of storytelling. That is, according to Luca Bandirali and Enrico Terrone, "narration is a normative notion in the sense that our cultural practices of appreciation involve some evaluative standards that allows us to establish whether a narration produces a well-formed narrative or not" (2017: 100).

episodes in the season (or series) are linked to each other through the existence of the same (main) characters that experience different—rarely connected—adventures in each episode.[60] We could also imagine a second case, wherein we have an anthology consisting of episodes that all refer to the overarching themes or world of the anthology. What relates the episodes are not the characters, but the theme of the anthology. An example of the first is a production like *The Simpsons* where from one episode to another we meet e.g. Homer Simpson. In the vast majority of episodes, he does not seem to be aware of what he has done in the previous shows. This allows us to think that the characters in *The Simpsons* are not aware of their psychological history. As an exemplar of anthology—as a second type of a strict series—we may include, for instance, *Black Mirror*. Here we have a list of episodes that present us new characters and storyline each time, but all the episodes refer somehow to the threat that stems from technological development and the uncertain future of humanity.

Television *non-continuous serials* is a mode of storytelling that is characterized by a closed number of episodes thematically and narratively linked to each other. From one episode to another, fictional characters provide new knowledge that helps the viewers understand the whole and immerses them in a plot that is developed through not one but many episodes. In this type of storytelling we enjoy the moral and psychological development of the fictional characters since they seem to be aware of their actions and intentions from the previous episodes. Non-continuous serials are limited to single season productions (e.g. *The Honourable Woman, Undercover*) or have a few seasons within productions (e.g. *No Offence, The Fall*). The classic examples of this kind of television narrative are serials such as *Mad Men* or *Hannibal*. Through several seasons (and years) the viewers witness the development, adventures, and moral decline of Peggy Olson and Don Draper or Dr Hannibal Lecter and Will Graham, respectively.

Television *continuous serials* as a module have much in common with non-continuous serials. They share, for example, the narrative and theme continuity between episodes, continuity where characters' development and morality grow, and the fact that fictional characters are "aware" of their actions and intentions from the previous episodes. There is one significant difference, however. Continuous serials are open-ended. Thus, they do not have a finite

60 A very good example of this type of television series are countless detective dramas focusing in each episode on different storyline (in particular, identifying a murderer and bringing him/her to justice).

number of episodes (cf. Geraghty 1981).[61] One of the most famous examples of this narrative mode is *The Bold and the Beautiful*. In this serial, airing since 1987, we are amused by the Forester family and their struggles with friends and enemies from the brutal fashion world. The never-ending story is full of dynamic and (quite often) absurd plot twists, such as deaths and "miraculous" resurrections.

For the purpose of this survey, the most important are non-continuous serials for which key examples are *The Wire, The Sopranos*, or *Twin Peaks*. Notwithstanding, even a cursory look at the series/serial distinction allows us to grasp the basic differences between the two modes of storytelling in television drama. Both modes suppose a sort of continuity between episodes (Oltean 1993: 14). Series create such continuity by using the same fictional characters from episode to episode or keeping tight thematic unity between the episodes. For example, all of the episodes remain in the horror or crime fiction genre. In such cases, we face different fictional characters every episode, but still there is a kind of continuity since the whole season is a profound study on some topic (e.g. the experience of lost). In the case of serials, we enjoy more literal continuity since not only protagonists and themes are continued but also the intentions of fictional characters.[62] What is more, series usually follow a linear narrative, whereas serials more often opt for a non-linear narrative. The reason for this division is that the plot in television series is limited to single episodes, and the viewers usually require fairly quick plot disclosure. TV serials work in the opposite way: the plot is extended for a number of episodes (and even seasons), so it is possible to create multileveled storylines. Not only the number of episodes and time passing between them is important but also a fictional space that allows characters to gain psychological complexity.[63]

The series/serial distinction should be understood as listing the two dominant trends within television storytelling. Of course, there are a considerable number of productions that fall completely into one side of that distinction, but there are also narrative hybrids that mix some characteristics of series and serials. There are TV serials that maintain strong links between episodes (characters, theme) while introducing one-shot stories into particular episodes. In

61 Naturally, this has quite a huge impact on the way in which narration is utilized in continuous serials. Such as the role of cliff-hangers, the organization of time, and the sense of a future—to name just a few. These interesting issues, however, are beyond the scope of this work.

62 For more, see section 5.2.

63 This is connected with the fact that, mostly, fictional characters in TV serials are "aware" of their previous actions and deeds. And, thus, they may shape their own decisions and behaviours according to what happened in the past.

other words, these TV series are defined by a meta-story that is extended to the whole production along with "small" stories that happen during each episode. (When these "small" stories are eventually linked together they form a meta-story). An example of a hybrid TV serial is *The Good Fight* which tells the story of a respected lawyer, Diane Lockhart, struggling with financial problems (*Nb.* she lost a substantial sum in her friend's financial scam). As a result, she is forced to put off her forthcoming retirement and remain professionally active. In the storyline we see numerous crimes and legal cases that are solved by Lockhart. There is also another multi-layer story present: the issue of her friend's guilt and investigating whether charges against him seem accurate or not.

5.2 Quasi-*causal Relations*

The basic formulation of a casual relation is "*A* causes *B*". This formulation assumes that a particular event (or object) is the cause of another other event (or object). Alternatively, it can be said that *A* is the cause of *B*, whereas *B* is the effect of *A*.[64] For the purpose of this study it is enough to say that television serials are based on the storyline continuity between episodes, and the relation between these episodes resembles causal relations in the real world.[65] That is, in television serials we have *quasi*-causal relations since it cannot be said strictly speaking—as with relations in natural sciences—that an event (or object) *A* causes event (or object) *B*. In other words, in Episode 2 of BBC's *McMafia* a young banker, Alex Goodman, decided to undertake money laundering for the Israeli politician Semiyon Kleiman, then in Episodes 4 & 5 the viewers witnessed the tragic consequences of Goodman's decision.

Acknowledging the existence of *quasi*-causal relations between episodes (and not just "inside" single episodes) in television serials is a form of fulfilling the categorial norm. In other words, all ontological and aesthetic research on television serials must take into account the presence of *quasi*-causal relations as well as the role they play in our experience of television dramas. The *quasi*-causal relations are a form of *extrinsic norms* that are imposed on this kind of storytelling by the medium of television. Fulfilling these norms is

64 For the purpose of this survey it is not necessary to determine in which framework we should interpret and understand causal relations between events or objects. We leave aside which description of the causal relation is more suitable—the ontological or epistemological one.

65 Cf. Ingarden (1979). Again, our point is valid whether the exact nature of fictional characters is determined or not. What is important is that fictional characters (even if real) exist in a different way than physical and spatio-temporal objects. See also Vidmar (2017).

important if the television drama belongs to the category of serials.[66] There are also intrinsic norms that are imposed by particular serials on themselves (cf. Mittell 2015: 44, 167–169). We claim that the existence and recognition of *quasi*-causal relations is crucial for establishing intrinsic norms that rule a particular television serial. Plot continuity and the importance of decisions made by characters (not always present in TV series) that extend particular episodes help to realize the *regularity* and provide a way of *fulfilling* intrinsic norms. The critical reception of TV serials to a certain extent depends on how the episodes (or seasons) cope with the norms and rules that are imposed by these serials.[67]

The importance of *quasi*-causal relations between episodes and the intrinsic norms highlighted by this relation can be seen in pilots and title sequences.

Two roles of pilots in television serials may be enumerated: educational and inspirational (cf. Mittell 2015: ch. 2). The first one amounts to the fact that through pilots we learn how to watch a given television serial. The second role refers to our sense of interest and immersion in the serial: the pilot must keep us glued to the screen and ensure that we will watch more episodes. Both roles are interconnected since discovering the way to (correctly) watch a TV serial increases the chances of further involvement in the serial. Both of these refer to the intrinsic norms of the TV serial that are established in the pilot. In the television serial the pilot is responsible for introducing fictional characters and revealing the relationships between them (even if changed dramatically through the dynamics of storytelling). Pilots teach us what we should and should not expect from the production. In other words, pilots serve as specific predictions for the whole serials. Naturally, pilots may differ from their serials in a myriad of superficial ways, but pilots are still a point of reference for the whole plot.[68] Thus, pilots are specific episodes that give you a chance to get the flavour of a TV serial's overall atmosphere.

The first episode of *Hannibal* is the epitome of how a television serial pilot works. The episode starts with scenes depicting a brutal murder of a couple. We see the working methods of FBI consultant Will Graham and how, thanks to an exceptionally high level of empathy, he is able to reconstruct the killer's actions and intentions. This process is likely to be described as deduction,

66 Otherwise, this norm would end up defining such objects as television *series* in the sense described above.

67 This refers to operational aesthetics—as explained in section 4.

68 A good example of such character development is *The Young Pope*. In the pilot we might get the impression that Pius XIII is very conservative as far as moral issues are concerned. However, through the whole serial we might notice that the pope—keeping his faith even more authentic and passionate—is becoming gradually more tolerant of homosexual priests or sees the huge importance of the feminine aspect in the Catholic Church.

and it is depicted as taking place "backwards". The viewers also get to know Graham's superior, Jack Crawford, who is deeply concerned about Graham's mental health and doubts in his ability to work in the field. As a result Will Graham is sent to Dr. Hannibal Lecter—a respected psychiatrist—for clinical consultations. At that moment, the character of Dr. Lecter is introduced as being in the middle of preparing a sophisticated dish. *Hannibal*'s pilot sets intrinsic norms for this TV serial; it establishes the manner of arranging the narrative and visual accents in the serial. It is easy to realize that the fictional characters are only inspired by Tomas Harris's *The Red Dragon*, as *Hannibal*'s characters are creatively developed in different ways from that of the novel. We are given a lot of information regarding Will Graham's working method as based on the primacy of vision, whereas Dr. Lecter is able to get valuable information from senses other than sight, e.g. taste or smell.[69] From the very beginning the viewers pay attention only to Dr. Lecter's relation to Graham and to the FBI as well as to everyday activities that are performed by Hannibal Lecter. This is especially true for scenes depicting food preparation and admiration of the arts. The pilot is an appetizer for the rest of the serial.[70]

Title sequences play a similar role to pilots, that is, they help to establish the intrinsic norms that govern the TV serial. However, title sequences work in a different way. The pilot is an integral yet special episode of the serial, whereas the title sequence is a constellation of images that is repetitively aired before each episode. Title sequences are the starting point for each episode, something that (at least, partly) creates TV serials' identity as well as a sort of dynamics and a reference point for each episode. (It is quite easy to notice which theme touched upon in the title sequence is realized or commented on in the episode). We would like to distinguish at least two types of title sequences:[71] (1) introducing fictional characters and (2) introducing themes.

The title sequence of MTV's supernatural teenage drama *Teen Wolf* is a nice example of the first type. The serial tells the story of Scott McCall and his friends from an American town called Beacon Hills. The protagonist is a werewolf, accompanied by friends gifted with supernatural powers, who tries to protect his beloved hometown from evil. Each of *Teen Wolf*'s six seasons bears a slightly different title sequence: they are created within the same structure, however. Each time, we see the main characters of the serial followed by the danger

69 For the role of sight in detective fiction see e.g. Weiss (2014), Horrowitz (1984), Hutter (1983).

70 *BN*. It is entitled—quite ironically—*Apéritif*.

71 Of course, the list is not (and, should not be) limited to these two types. We are just noting a particular tendency within title sequences.

that threatens the town. The representation of the main characters changes over time, such that new powers and alliances are always reflected in the title sequence. A different version of this type of title sequence can be found in the teenage drama *Skins*. The main characters are teenagers that experience school dramas, romances, and growing up in Bristol. Each episode is devoted to a different character (or a pair of characters) and *Skins*' title sequence anticipates that fact. In the sequence of camera shots, the leading character of the episode is set off. The title sequences of both serials remind us of teenagers' unstable identity and show how it is embodied in the ongoing programme.

True Blood is an example of the second type of title sequence. This HBO television serial tells the story of vampires in contemporary USA. After inventing and distributing "artificial blood" called true blood, vampires decided to come out and live peacefully among humans. *True Blood*'s title sequence does not introduce any particular fictional characters but rather allows us to get a sense of the serial's overall theme (the title sequence remains unchanged through all of its seasons). The themes covered in the serial are, among others, fanatic religiosity and its destructive influence on social otherness, brutality, crime, and sexual desires. Special attention is given to ongoing social problems such as discrimination of sexual minorities. One of the scenes shows a billboard that reads "God hates fangs", a play on slogans touted by some organizations against same sex marriage.

Pilots and title sequences work in different ways, but at a fundamental level important similarities between them can be found. Actions undertaken by characters have consequences (granted by *quasi*-casual dependence) throughout a serial. Between episodes we may find narrative links and continuity. Their relationships seem to be crucial for the fulfilment of intrinsic norms in television serials. We may say that these norms are satisfied only if there is a connection between episodes. Pilots and title sequences, through introducing fictional characters, narrative techniques, themes, and stylistic conventions, are able to disclose many of the intrinsic norms governing a given TV serial.

5.3 *Temporal Relations*

Time is one of the most crucial factors describing television serials.[72] Together with such parameters as characters, events, and space, time is necessary for fragmentarization of the narrative (Mittell 2015: 263). Time is responsible

72 Time is essential for every narrative since it allows for exploitation of its fictional world. In the case of television series and serials, the vast amount of narrative time invites complex development of characters and plot. However, interestingly, in some cases these amounts of time become a problem for television dramas. See Bandirali and Terrone (2017).

for the redundancy of narrative events, and it also plays a significant role in our experience of television dramas. It is instructive to enumerate a few notions of time that are of great importance when studying television narratives (ibid.: 26). *Story time* refers to the time that is passing within the story world (this is usually a linear model of time passing). *Discourse time* defines how the passing of time is depicted in a television serial.[73] Very often this is a nonlinear module because in television dramas many narrative techniques relate to time such as introspections—involving flashes from the past and the future. Disclosing the way in which discourse time is presented is often integral to understanding the intrinsic norms of a particular narrative. Lastly, there is *screen time*. It is the temporal format in which we experience television serials. Screen time is strictly defined by the TV company that airs the television serial. Usually, episodes last between 30 to 60 minutes each and are aired in weekly intervals.

For the purposes of this survey, we shall focus primarily on screen time. Not only because it is the format that has the biggest influence on our experience of television dramas, but also because it facilitates the existence of the specific relations between episodes. As has been pointed out, these relations are *quasi*-causal in nature. Moreover, quasi-causal relations happen in a temporal framework. That is, they are characterized by a specific dynamic. This dynamic is vital for our experience of television serials as well as for understanding what television serials really are. Thus, in this part of the survey we are interested in narrative connections between episodes that happen in a temporal framework of passing time. The temporal relations between episodes influence extrinsic and intrinsic norms as experienced by the viewers. This is because the regularity of fulfilling these norms is embodied not only in discourse time but also in real time. For example, if the intrinsic norm of a given TV serial suggests that every single episode starts from scenes depicting death and funeral preparations (*Six Feet Under*), then it matters that all this happens every week at a regular time. Regularity and repeatability of narrative elements foster their understanding and experience. The same goes for quasi-causal relations between episodes. The fact that an action undertaken in Episode 2 has consequences in Episode 5 (so, roughly, 3 weeks later) helps us better internalize that these episodes are *really* connected. We do not claim, however, that within the body

---

73 We follow Chatman's understanding of these terms. Namely, "a story (*histoire*), [is] the content or chain of events (actions, happenings), plus what may be called the existents (characters, items of setting); and a discourse (*discours*), that is the expression, the means by which the content is communicated. In simple terms, the story is what in a narrative *that* is depicted, discourse the *how*" (1978: 19).

of TV serials (ontologically speaking) we should include the time passed between episodes. We also do not argue that what happens to the TV serials' text between episodes should be taken into account as an ontological part of TV serials.[74] We do claim that temporal intervals between episodes have an influence on how the story is created and told.

Of course, fictional characters are what we value most in television dramas.[75] We frequently keep our fingers crossed for their choices, experience deep disappointments with them, and witness their moral development or decline. The possibility of change—no matter how we understand the nature of this change, as development or accumulation—is an important feature responsible for characters' authenticity and identity (Pearson 2008: 55–56). We all change, and the same happens to our beloved characters. This all happens in time, obviously. One of the inevitable consequences of seriality and temporal intervals[76] between episodes is that the viewers often forget many things regarding their television dramas. For example, characters' names, places, events as well as emotional states and intentions motivating the protagonists. The process of forgetting is anticipated and tacitly involved in the very nature of television narratives since many TV series are aired for a number of years.[77]

Recognition of, and emotional identification with, fictional characters requires a substantial amount of knowledge. Again, the creators of TV serials are aware of that. The vast majority of productions are opened with a section restating what happened in the previous episodes ("previously on ..."). The montage includes not only what happened in the last few episodes but can even refer to the very beginning of the serial. The chronology of events presented in the "previously on" does not necessarily overlap the chronology of the events that happened in the whole serial (in terms of story time). Quite often the "previously on" section is a creative rearrangement of events that mix characters and the relations between them.[78] This invites us to search for

74 See section 6.

75 See e.g. Smith (1995), Eder (2010), Eder, Jannidis, and Schnelder (2010).

76 For the purposes of this study, it is taken for granted that episodes are watched by viewers within the constraints of a television network—for example, weekly. However, there are also different formats allowing the viewers to watch episodes without such strictly defined temporal intervals. For more details, see section 6.

77 Note that—apart from the usual seasons—more and more serials have been adopting so-called mid-seasons.

78 The function of recaps ("previously on" sections) is in fact quite complex in itself. They might serve as (1) a mechanism of reinterpretation of the existing plotline, (2) a summary of what happened before, or (3) a reopening of narrative fragments from previous episodes or seasons. Recaps give relevance to some scenes that are continued within the series, as well as guide us through the overall narration. An excellent piece of scholarship

new interpretations of the plot but also may be a predictor of what will happen in the episode. It is clear how important events from early episodes can be, since they have some non-trivial continuations or consequences in later episodes. Past events also help the viewers recall intrinsic norms embodied in television serials.

An interesting example of the described montage technique is presented in the critically acclaimed serial entitled *Shameless* (US production). The recapitulation of previous events is always accompanied by a commentary from the members of the Gallagher family. Usually, we "encounter" one of the Gallaghers when s/he is doing something referring to the last episode. When the character "notices" us she or he yells at us or makes some other fuss about why we did not have time to watch the last episode. And then the character says: "Here is what you've missed last week!". The opening scenes of *Shameless* show that its creators are fully aware—through the projected awareness of the fictional characters—that the viewers have a bad habit: skipping an episode or two. The Gallagher family regularly yelling at the viewers about not watching the show last time builds up an impression that viewership is a kind of duty. That is, we are obligated to keep up with what is happening to the Gallaghers. One interpretation says that if we really want to be close to our beloved characters, we must let them into our lives and treat them as a part of our everyday.[79]

Story time that passes between episodes is an element defining the nature of television serials. A change in story time assumes that discourse time is passing as well (the same is true, of course, with screen time). It is not very rare to see serious alterations in narratives between seasons. This may suggest that during the time passing—story time *and* screen time—revolutionary changes took place. The viewers are exposed to such a situation when watching *Hannibal*. In the last season we are informed that Dr. Alana Bloom is in a romantic relationship with Margot Vernes. Such a serious plot twist shows that both story and discourse time is passing, even if the serial is not being aired.[80]

5.4 *Episodes in Order*

Acknowledging that quasi-causal and temporal relations are important for understanding the ontological nature of television serials has its own consequences. Namely, we are committed to a certain view about the relationships

---

devoted to the role of recaps in television dramas (using *Breaking Bad* as a case study) is provided in Dusi (2016).

79 Regularity is an important factor in everyday aesthetics. Cf. Melchionne (2013). See also Naukkarinen (2017).

80 See also Oltean (1993).

that obtain between episodes and the whole (a season or a serial as such). Seasons in television serials are closed units consisting of sequences of orderly structured episodes. There are temporal and *quasi*-causal relations between episodes themselves. This means that each episode is interpreted as referring to the others. In particular, the later episodes are experienced as on the horizon of the earlier ones. However, an objection to this statement might be formulated on the grounds that some episodes enjoy such a degree of unity and plot disclosure that it is perfectly coherent to think of them as separate works. If so, then these episodes might be judged as separated entities or as parts of the larger whole.[81] Thus, it seems that despite the existence of *quasi*-causal and temporal relations there is a kind of autonomy granted to some episodes. Good candidates for such privileged episodes are pilots and so-called bottle episodes (specific episodes that are situated "out of" the main storyline). The objection, despite its intuitive appeal, can be easily neutralized.

It is true that pilots are privileged episodes in television serials. They last longer than regular episodes, are directed by prominent artists, consist of a number of intriguing plot twists, and introduce viewers to the new world and characters. The key characteristic that seems to make pilots good candidates for autonomous episodes is the fact that there is nothing before them. Pilots are not the "result" of episodes that happened before. However, it should be noted that pilots are meant to be starting points for television narratives. Moreover, pilots are very often judged as a beginning and if so, then pilots refer to something (episodes) that comes after them. It is only in such cases that we are able to judge if they are successful. (Where "successfulness" is taken to mean a high rating or the fact that the serial is still aired).

Bottle episodes are somehow similar to pilots. For example, when watching *Breaking Bad*'s episode called "Fly" the viewers may think that the episode is beyond or out the main storyline. (In short: during the episode, Walter and Jessie try to neutralize a fly that accidentally flew into the laboratory). Also, bottle episodes quite often use stylistics or narrative conventions that differ from those adopted in the serial. They seem to somehow exist beyond *quasi*-causal relations, and yet it is hard to treat them as fully autonomous episodes. This so is because bottle episodes are defined on the horizon of earlier episodes. How they function outside the main storyline is only evident when the viewers are able to recognize and appreciate the otherness of these episodes.

Taking the above into account, we shall suggest that pilots and bottle episodes cannot be treated *simultaneously* as (1) entities autonomous from the

81 Some intuitions supporting this point of view might be found in Mittell (2015: 74) and Nannicelli (2012: 176–178).

other episodes and (2) parts of the greater whole. For example, if a pilot is understood and experienced as autonomous from the episodes that follow, then it is more like a film production.[82] That is so because the episodes in serials (as defined in this study) are always connected to each other. Even if an episode has an exceptionally tense plot unity and successful plot disclosure, it is still a part of something more since it is defined *as* an episode.[83] The situation is analogous in terms of bottle episodes. Their extraordinariness is defined relative to the regular episodes.

In this part of the survey the ontological nature of television serials has been outlined. The next part is devoted to establishing how the hierarchy of norms facilitates aesthetic experience of television drama. Then, after discussing the relevance of the categorial norm, the aesthetic norm will be elaborated in detail.

6 The Aesthetics of Watching

6.1 *Normativity of Reception*

TV series owe their cultural and academic importance to, among other things, the force of their aesthetic impact. Seriality, no matter how it is construed, would have been much less interesting, if it had been possible to treat it solely as a feature that defines a class of artefacts. It would have been less noteworthy because its range would have been narrower, which does not mean that it would have been less significant.[84]

It may be, however, said that seriality—regardless of whether it defines 19th-century novels, comic books, or TV series—goes beyond the structure or form of particular works, determining numerous audience practices that are *raison d'être* of these works. This is one of the reasons why numerous studies (if not the majority of them) focus on ways in which TV series are watched and interpreted (incidentally, this corresponds to the market reality governed by viewing figures).

82 This thesis applies to critical practice and not to metaphysics. It is *very* hard to treat an episode at the same time as both an autonomous entity from other episodes and as a part of a larger whole.

83 This claim does not undermine the statement that every part (e.g. an episode) of serial art (e.g. a TV serial) is a work of art in itself. See Mag Uidhir (2013).

84 The debates on television as art or on the criteria of quality TV prove that seriality is worthy of attention even when it is conceived of mainly as a factor decisive for production and distribution.

Our claim is that the normativity implied by seriality and hitherto discussed on the ontological level also applies to how TV series are watched. Of course, the contention that the reception of TV series is subject to norms rooted in their structure may sound even more dubitable than the idea of creative normativity, especially when one has in mind the gamut of post-structuralist theories. Nonetheless, we believe that the reception of TV series is defined by norms just as making them is defined by them, in the sense that if someone's intention is to create a TV series, then she has to give her filmic work a serial structure which is such that no matter what formal or diegetic experiments are used, it will be possible to locate it somewhere in the continuum between a TV series and a serial. In order to appreciate the experimental aspects of a television series, one has to recognize, above all, that one is watching a TV series, i.e. one has to fulfil the categorial norm. Therefore, just as it is possible to think of standard, variable, and contra-standard properties of TV series which allow one to recognize them as serial shows, so too *per analogiam* one may think of standard, variable, and contra-standard factors which allow one to decide whether a certain way of watching a TV series may be considered "watching a TV series (as a TV series)" or not and, consequently, whether such a reception allows the viewer to fulfil the aesthetic norm.

We claim that aesthetic reception is always governed by the aesthetic norm which, we believe, is intuitive and defines our desire to get the fullest aesthetic satisfaction possible regardless of its source, be it a book, a piece of music, film (a TV series), or wine. Avoiding fulfilling the aesthetic norm is theoretically possible, but it seems to contradict common sense and practice (even a post-structuralist one) and resembles an effort to finish a marathon run in last place.

The controversy over normativity of reception does not refer to the idea of aesthetic norm which is unanimously assumed, at least implicitly, but to the idea of categorial norm. Post-structuralists deny its existence, claiming that one does not need it in order to—as Stanley Fish (1980) would have it—"recognize a TV series when one sees it", whereas non-post-structuralists contend that it is indispensable, for one has to know what one is experiencing in the first place in order to relate to it in any way.[85]

The aesthetic norm is, as we stated above, genetically dependent on the categorial one in the sense that the more one aims at fulfilling the former, the more efficiently one has to fulfil the latter. Of course, it is conceivable—and in fact this is very often the case—to watch a pilot without watching the TV series it introduces, or to watch only the first episode or one in the middle, and to get

85 On this topic see Nannicelli (2016).

aesthetic satisfaction out of it, but this sort of satisfaction will not be like the one obtained from watching a TV series as a whole structured by non-trivial seriality.

We do intend to fetishize the whole as an autonomous, closed structure conceived of as an aesthetic ideal in which every single element occupies its place and thus has a fixed sense, but we want to underline that even if the whole—just like the episodes of a TV serial, contrary to the episodes of a TV series—is open and inconclusive because it is "hyperdiegetic" (Hill 2004) or created in a Romantic vein as "incomplete, fragmentary and inherently unstable" (Jacobs 2001: 444), it is a sort of horizon which one should account for if one wants one's reception of it to be more rewarding. It is only in light of its serial character that a TV series may reveal its aesthetic richness to the fullest and thus allow its viewers to achieve a greater aesthetic satisfaction, i.e. to better fulfil the aesthetic norm.

The categorial norm tells us, then, to recognize that we are watching e.g. a pilot or the third episode of the second season, but above all that it is an episode which belongs to a serial whole and hence its appreciation and interpretation depends on whether it is seen in light of the whole it is a part of. So, the categorial norm implies that we should watch the whole TV series because only then can we experience its seriality. What is more, the categorial norm implies that we should recognize the character of seriality, whether it is a continuous or non-continuous drama and—above all—whether it is a TV series, a TV serial, or a hybrid form.[86]

In other words, the categorial norm tells us to take into consideration seriality together with its type and all the consequences it may have for what we watch and how we watch it. Let us indicate two of them. First, it implies that we should not appreciate a pilot "vertically" as a single, stand-alone work, but "horizontally" (Aprile 2010), i.e. as announcing the TV series. Second, it indicates that if we started watching a TV series from the middle, we should watch the episodes we missed but at the same time we should be aware that even if we manage to get an overall view of the show, our satisfaction will be different than the satisfaction we would have had, had we watched it right from the beginning. The difference will be due not only to the fact that *nolens volens* we violated the chronology of the narrative, but also to our omitting the temporal aspect of the TV series, namely the fact that episodes are usually watched one or two at a time, which is usually thought to significantly heighten the viewers' aesthetic satisfaction. Recognition of the serial structure is, then, accompanied

86 The categorial norm has larger implications which are, however, outside the scope of the article, e.g. it implies that the genre of TV drama be recognized as well.

consequently, may be qualified as "non-reading", which prevents one from complying with aesthetic norms. According to Bayard (2012), who contends that reading implies non-reading, such an approach is far from obvious, as the answer to the question "what does it mean to read a book?" is subject to various social and aesthetic norms. Binge watching raises a similar question—"what does it mean to watch a TV series?" We are not going to discuss *a la* Bayard whether watching a TV series implies non-watching it, but we will come back to the issue of the binge watchers' aesthetic norm in a while.

Various other fan practices are also believed to dent seriality, especially those which stem from a particular intellectual and emotional engagement in TV series. Although fan activities are concentrated on TV series, they are not limited solely to watching them—fans enlarge the fictive world shown in them in various ways so that it tends to merge with real life. Not only do they comment on TV series using social media or speculate on what will happen in forthcoming episodes (sometimes even effectively influencing the decisions of TV series creators), but they are also willing to allude to their favourite protagonists in their daily practices, creating fan communities or "neo-tribes" (Bonazzi 2001: 116) based on TV series considered by them to be cult.[91] As a result, seriality becomes more and more transmedial.[92] Practices rooted in fan culture and transmediality tend to be treated as activities that undermine traditional seriality in so far as they belong to a culture based on participatory practices; hence, they conceive of seriality not as an established order to be obeyed, but as a structure that fosters free activities that are very often determined not by what is shown in a TV series but by what happens beyond it, in other media.

If binge watching is said to deconstruct seriality by interfering with its "temporal dilatation", fan practices are believed to do the same by weakening seriality as a factor that determines the ontology of TV series.

6.3 *The Implied Viewer*

The abovementioned technological changes which allow anyone to watch a number of episodes at any time and in any order, as well as new modes of distribution (e.g. whole seasons are offered at once), made some scholars coin such terms as "post-seriality" (Brancato 2011) or "post-broadcast era" (Keinonen 2016). One could say that what has changed is the shape of the categorial norm, if we understand it as a norm which tells us to watch episodes in the order and at the intervals intended by the creators of TV series together with the broadcasters because it is the best way to get maximum aesthetic satisfaction.

91 On cult TV see e.g. Abbott (2010), Gwenllian-Jones and Pearsons (2004), Lavery (2010).

92 On this topic see e.g. Evans (2011), Keinonen (2016), Mittell (2015).

What is more, in light of contemporary fan practices, the idea of categorial norm may appear to be one which should be dismissed as an expression of obsolete watching practices that do not correspond in any way to current social and technological reality as well as of an outdated model of reception governed by a certain aesthetic ideal. In other words, the categorial norm may appear to be construed on the basis of an old standard of production, distribution, and consumption and to serve now as a criterion for evaluating various ways of watching TV series. This is not the view we want to endorse, as we understand the normativity implied by the categorial norm in a different manner.

In order to explain how we conceive of the normativity of reception, we would like to adapt to our needs the typology of standard, variable, and contra-standard aesthetic properties and to use the idea of "the implied viewer" (Kozloff 2005), i.e. the viewer to whom a TV series is dedicated to and who is in a certain way created by it. As Helen Fulton writes:

> When we consider the audiences for media texts, it seems obvious that in a literal sense they are people like us, watching television, going to the movies, buying newspapers. But from a theoretical perspective, an audience is called into being by a particular discourse, or 'interpellated' by the text, to use Althusser's term. In other words, an audience doesn't exist until a text addresses it; and by the same token, texts don't simply address a pre-existing and knowable audience.
>
> FULTON 2005: 5

We define the implied viewer as a viewer who is able to fully fulfil the categorial norm and the aesthetic norm accordingly. We contend, then, that the reception of such an implied viewer defines what we shall call the standard reception (the standard way of watching a TV series). A contra-standard reception is, therefore, one that does not comply in any way with the categorial norm and the corresponding way of complying with the aesthetic norm. That a contra-standard approach denies the possibility of fulfilling the aesthetic norm in the way implied by seriality does not mean that one cannot do in some other way. An example of a contra-standard reception is watching a TV series "backwards" or watching episodes in a random order. The distinction between standard and contra-standard reception is not supposed to lead to the claim that contra-standard ways of watching TV series should be considered wrong or preposterous and as such avoided, but to underline that they are in contrast with those that we still consider "standard".

Although technological changes and corresponding changes in watchers' habits have cause the traditional way of watching TV series defined in the "broadcast era" to become nothing more than one of many possibilities, this sort of reception may still be considered the standard one.[93] The reason for this is that it is implied by seriality, which still defines TV series even if they are distributed in a non-traditional way different from the ritualized version of broadcasting or if their creators tempt their audience to watch them in contra-standard manners. An issue that requires empirical study is how many people in fact watch them in a contra-standard way, for it involves, among other things, the risk of losing one of the greatest pleasures that TV series may give people, namely the one rooted in expectations as to what is going to happen next. As John Ellis (2001: 151) notices: "the deliciousness of the anticipation is worth in many instances more than the event itself. Speculation abounds; the event is perfunctory."

One cannot exclude that in the future—and if this is going to happen, it will certainly occur sooner than later—there will be mainstream production of TV series that will resemble such novels as Julio Cortazar's *Hopscotch* or poems such as Raymond Queneau's *A Hundred Thousand Billion Poems* and will invite the audience to contra-standard reception. An important question arises here whether such TV series would still be TV series or not, given that they would not possess standard properties of TV series. It seems that they would not, as their ontology would be different. Or rather, if they were to be considered TV series, seriality itself should be defined in some other way, which would amount to giving up the concept of seriality we are referring to throughout the paper. Nevertheless, even then it would be possible to claim that the categorial and aesthetic norms exist and that it would be possible to distinguish standard, variable, and contra-standard ways of watching.

No matter what the future of TV series will be like, current contra-standard manners of watching them are contra-standard in the sense that they are hardly ever practiced. It should be noticed that the supposed deconstructing practices mentioned above, such as binge watching, are not to be considered contra-standard, because they comply with the categorial norm in that they respect the rule that all the episodes should be watched in the order intended by the creators of the TV series and that they should be watched as episodes of a serial drama. At the same time, however, they transgress this norm inasmuch as they do not respect the time gaps between episodes, which were once

93 One could notice that a major difference between watching TV series in the "broadcast era" and in post-broadcast times lies in the fact that it is now possible to watch them without advertisements. However, even if they are in fact absent, one may still figure out where they once were or where they could be—it is very often suggested by the structure of episodes divided into smaller "wholes".

imposed by creators and broadcasters and are still treated, to some extent, as default even if they are not clearly defined. Otherwise, why should one feel guilty when watching more than one or two episodes at a time? Binge watching allows one to appreciate seriality conceived of as the narrative structure described above, based on "the time of the told, [but also] the time of the telling", yet it overlooks "the time of the broadcasting". Respecting the intervals between episodes as a "property" of watching TV series is then analogous to variable properties of an object, i.e. properties which are insignificant in terms of classifying it as such-and-such object.

In other words, whether a TV series is binge watched or watched *comme il faut* has no impact on whether it is watched as a TV series or not, provided that the categorial norm is fulfilled otherwise. The fact that, for example, one could watch a whole season of *The Wired* in one day, does not prevent one from recognizing its serial character. It may be added that even binge watchers are well aware that they are watching something whose seriality is intended to be consumed "little by little" and not "bulimically".

Yet another question is whether omitting the gaps between episodes determines the degree to which the aesthetic norm is fulfilled. It seems that it does, at least to a certain extent, because aesthetic satisfaction stems not only from following the narrative shown in subsequent episodes, but also from what may happen during the intervals between them. As Ellis notes, anticipation may be more important than the events shown in TV series, and anticipation, like interest, suspense, and other emotions, caused by what one saw in an episode may appear and mature between the end of one episode and the beginning of the next. The time between the episodes may be filled with ruminations, speculations, exchanges of ideas or opinions on what has already happened in a TV series or what is yet to come. If seriality favours "getting into it", it does so not only because it facilitates the creation of a complex story which may be found more intriguing by the audience, but also because in its most traditional form it gives the audience enough time to get engaged in it in various ways, from commenting in social media, playing related games, buying periodicals, to emulating the protagonists or—in some cases—deciding on what is going to happen to them. The fact that such engagement is usually not fully spontaneous, as it is designed by the creators of TV series, is of little importance here.

Contemporary TV series may be so successfully transmedial due to the intervals between episodes—they do not converge with other media after they end but, more often than not, when they are still "on the air". Seen from this point of view, fan practices are far less untraditional than they may appear at first sight. Although one could argue that transmediality inevitably destroys seriality, ultimately it does not have to be so. For example, many people do not want to have their favourite TV serial spoilt by others telling them what will happen in the forthcomings episodes or how the season will end. And even though they may easily find all of that out by themselves thanks to the internet, they tend to refrain from doing so. Of course, there are TV fans who wish to know the finale in advance, but this knowledge may only help them in appreciating the type of seriality used in a TV series.[94]

Fandom is thought to be participatory as fans are not passive beholders who solely "absorb" what is offered to them by the creators of TV series, but active interpreters who do different things with TV series. Hence, TV series are often said to be co-created by them.[95] This results in conceiving of TV series in post-structuralist terms as e.g. texts similar to galaxies whose boundaries and properties are not defined once and for all and largely depend on the interpreter's decision, interests, aims etc. A TV series and its elements are thus said to lose their identity.[96]

Willingly agreeing with the view that fans are active, we would like to point out that their practices very often take place between episodes and do not influence their identity, in the sense that the structure of a TV series remains intact. Hence, it remains unchanged despite being placed in various contexts—foreseen by the creators or not—where it may start to function in such a way that produces meanings not intended by its creators. If we believe that seriality involves not only "the time of the told" and "the time of the telling", but also "the time of the watching" (our expression), then seriality turns out to foster fan practices.

In other words, in order to fulfil the aesthetic norm according to their own tastes, fans tend to develop their activities between episodes, yet they do not fail the categorial norm.[97] Quite the contrary, as they may be said to do it in a more rigorous way than others, for this ensures that they obtain more material for the actions they undertake when they are not watching episodes; thus, they can get more aesthetic satisfaction. This is what creators aim at when they create TV series that invite fan practices, i.e. series whose implied viewer is a fan-viewer.

94 On the topic of spoilers see e.g. Brojakowski (2015), Mittell (2015: 174–177).

95 On fan culture see e.g. Booth (2018), Click and Scott (2017), Geraghty (2015), Hills (2002).

96 See Nannicelli (2016: 88–121).

97 Examples of such activities are: looking for information about the protagonists, commenting on the show, imitating heroes' clothing, ways of talking, etc.

6.4 *Post-seriality and Normativity*

Although any general claim about TV is questionable given that series have been evolving as fast as the technical means of their production and distribution as well as the social practices within which they appear, it may be contended that seriality has remained essentially unchanged and that it is therefore possible to discuss the norms governing such a protean and unpredictable sphere as reception.

TV series require a sort of engagement and create a sort of aesthetic satisfaction different than non-serial films do. Viewers get engaged in TV series—and once they are engaged, they want their engagement to be continued—because TV series entice them to do so in two ways. First, the audience is offered time gaps between the episodes and it depends only on viewers' discretion whether they will make use of them or not. Second, narratives shown in TV series require an intellectual investment on behalf of the audience in order to be understood and appreciated. The engagement discussed here may undoubtedly have different forms and varied extent, yet it is always determined by seriality.[98]

The normativity of reception is particularly questionable where cult TV series are concerned. It is true that

> cult television's serial and segmented forms, its familiar formulae, its accumulated multiple storylines, its metatextuality, its ubiquitous intertextuality and intra-textuality, its extension across a variety of other media, its modes of self-reflexivity and constant play of interruption and excess, work together to overwhelm the processual order of cause and effect, enigma and resolution, extending story events and other narrative and textual elements across boundless networks of interconnected possibilities.
>
> GWENLLIAN-JONES AND PEARSONS 2004: XVII

At the same time, however, the "boundless networks of interconnected possibilities" in which the viewer moves are defined by seriality in the sense that "cult TV's hyperdiegesis [...] works serially, by reiteration and by accumulation of detail" (Hills 2004: 511). As a result, the viewer gradually gets more and more information and thus can more and more easily move around in this network. Thus, the "interactivity" of TV series, which is believed to undermine

98 Seriality is also important where phenomena such as post-fandom are concerned, i.e. fan practices that take place when a TV series is over (Williams 2015).

the idea of seriality, has a sequential character itself (Allrath, Gymnich, and Surkat 2005: 10).[99]

In other words, even practices that are deemed deconstructionist do not really weaken seriality, and hence such expressions as "post-seriality" are meaningful only in so far as they refer to seriality as an object of contemporary practices that depart from the watching customs typical of the era when TV series could only be watched on television. The fact that post-seriality breaks with tradition in this sense does not make it contra-standard, at least for now.

Post-seriality is thus linked to practices enabled by new technologies offering unlimited access to TV series and other media. In fact, the greatest change these new conditions have made in TV series distribution consists in giving today's viewers an opportunity to intentionally control aesthetic satisfaction, 'which is derivable from their capacity to wait before they watch a new episode and thereby engage in what is inherent to the "default mode of perception" (ibid.: 8). These new reception practices are based on the usage of sources other than TV series themselves, which for many viewers are an indispensable means of heightening their aesthetic satisfaction. Post-seriality should be, then, associated with certain modes of fulfilling the aesthetic norm—binge watching together with its bulimic pleasure or transmediatic fan practices accompanied by their "complex" pleasures are examples of such "post-serial" manners. In both cases, however, the categorial norm is still in force, as one should recognize that one is watching a TV series, i.e. a film whose seriality is non-trivial—one binge watches a TV series and not a film that simply lasts many hours. Similarly, we can play with intertextual, transmedial, etc. aspects or elements of TV series, nonetheless they keep appearing successively, from one episode to another, which significantly determines how we can "play" with them not by limiting the number of possibilities at one's disposal, but by gradually opening new ones.

One could agree that "seriality no longer offers a linear sequence of events, but instead an a-linear flexible sequence of information, each piece of which enriches the viewer, listener, or reader's ability to re-interpret the central events" (Kustritz 2014, 233). In order to express one's consent, however, one would have to change the way seriality and TV series are understood. The question arises whether such a change of definition would not amount to overlooking what is unanimously believed to be so interesting and valuable about them. It seems in fact that it would render seriality trivial; seriality would cease

99 In order to be successful, transmedia practices follow "the time of broadcasting" (Keinonen 2016).

to be a feature of TV series despite being what so profoundly distinguishes them from other television shows.

7 Conclusion

Televisions series are serial audio-visual narratives. The phenomenon of seriality can be understood both as a mode of narration and a mode of distribution.[100] The first reading of seriality means that a single story, regardless of its complexity, can be fragmented into smaller units. Each unit alone is an episode, whereas a sequence of episodes is a season. Serial television dramas are narrative works that achieve plot unity and disclosure through sequences of episodes. The second understanding of seriality amounts to the fact that television dramas are broadcasted in episodes that create seasons, and this broadcasting is structured into repeatable and regular timeframes (e.g. weekly). Thanks to its specificity, seriality has a significant influence on narrative works that employ this form of narration and distribution. The purpose of this study was to investigate the relationship between TV series (taken as serial narrative dramas) and normativity. We have achieved this goal through a detailed survey of the concept of seriality in culture and the arts as well as by linking that concept with a philosophically oriented understanding of norms, ontology, and aesthetics.

In terms of ontology, television series are narrative entities that are grouped into larger wholes—seasons or completed productions. We have shown that the ontology of television series is based on non-trivial seriality which, practically speaking, implies two kinds of relations between narrative contents of episodes: quasi-causal relations and temporal relations. Also, it has been suggested that one of the consequences of the existence of such relations is the narrative structure of single episodes. Namely, a single episode cannot be treated simultaneously as an autonomous artwork and a part of a greater narrative whole. We have also sketched the aesthetics of television series. In particular, we focused on the aesthetics of viewers' reception rather than on listing the possible formal aesthetic properties exemplified by TV series. It has been noted that television series create a specific kind of viewer engagement. That is, the viewers must invest some intellectual effort in order to experience television dramas in a truly rewarding way. Aesthetic reception and appreciation of television series demand a different kind of attention than is present

100 Note that these two ways in which seriality can be understood are not mutually exclusive. It is rather the opposite. They refer to different aspects of the same phenomenon.

with cinematic works. Since series are fragmented into episodes, viewers do not get full plot disclosure in a single episode[101] and must reconstruct the narrative from the fragments (episodes).

We have established the ontology and aesthetics of TV series as rooted in the relationship between two special kinds of norms. We presented and discussed the two norms: the categorial norm and the aesthetic norm. Recall that: for an artwork *x* the first norm says that we should discover *x*'s categories, ontological nature, and sanctions put upon *x*, whereas the second norm calls for maximalisation of *x*'s aesthetic impact. The relation between the norms is a normative one. That is, we establish a hierarchy which says that fulfilling the categorial norm is both theoretically and practically more important than fulfilling the aesthetic one. It is so due to the fact that the categorial norm forces us to define and establish the real object of our (aesthetic) inquiry. Without this, it would be hard to fulfil the aesthetic norm since this norm refers to the maximalisation of *x*'s aesthetic impact if and only if we know that *x* really is. However, it must be noted that the reason motivating fulfilling the categorial norm is aesthetic interest. In other words, if we follow the categorial norm, we do it because we would like to experience *x* correctly, i.e. as non-trivially serial. It is also possible to fulfil the aesthetic norm in other manners, but any such contra-standard approach will lead to an aesthetic satisfaction that has nothing—or at least very little—to do with the fact that its source is a non-trivially serial work.

Philosophical aesthetics is the perspective adopted in this study. It might be noted that the outcome of this survey could also be reached by other academic disciplines such as media theory or cultural studies. That is hard to deny, since the mentioned disciplines are deeply interested in seriality as a historical convention that is embodied in a vast number of frameworks: arts, politics, economics to name just a few. Agreeing with this approach, it must be mentioned that philosophical aesthetics gives another perspective. While the historicity of seriality is not denied, the philosophical perspective is more interested in investigations of the atemporal structure of seriality as *differentia specifica* of certain TV shows. That is, philosophy is more interested in the conceptual framework and the logical relationships between concepts rather than taking a close look at particular TV series' contents or listing social determinants of television narratives.

There are at least three major interrelated objections to our approach that can be put forward by exponents of philosophical aesthetics as well as series studies scholars. First, we may be easily accused of universalism, as the

101 We mean here a meta-story that is extended into the whole season. See section 5.

normativity we describe is in fact global, which is highly debatable. Cultural studies scholars may remark, and justly so, that TV series are created and watched in so many social contexts that the only norms that exist—if they exist at all—are expressions of the local history of television culture and its present conditions. Second, media theorists may in turn claim, again not without reason, that our approach is essentialist, as we intentionally ignore history. As a result they may hold that we illegitimately assume one standard of seriality, dismissing works which do not comply with it or deeming some works better than others in so far as they fall closer to our ideal of seriality, i.e. non-trivial seriality as typical of "pure" serials. These two objections may be added together in order to put forward the third one, namely that the seriality we are interested in is based on the type of seriality used by quality TV (or complex TV) and that we consequently reproduce a hegemonic aesthetic canon.

In order to answer the first objection, we would like to point out that seriality is sometimes discussed as a genre, a format, or a form.[102] The body of literature on TV series is full of definitions of these concepts which are considered useful as analytical tools despite referring to a gamut of phenomena functioning in social contexts that may make them quite dissimilar.[103] The claim that it is possible to offer a definition of seriality covering all TV series should not then strike one as odd or debatable. Just as the idea of genre may be said to be commonsensical to a certain degree (Dunn 2005), so too seriality can be considered such, which is proved by e.g. fan and non-fan practices. In fact, practically no one has difficulties with recognizing that they are watching a TV series.

Given that the term *genre* refers to stylistic features of works as well as their content (it is possible to discuss various genres of TV series), whereas *format* denotes a ready-to-use formula and refers to legal and economic issues related to its usage (a TV series may be formatted),[104] we would like to suggest that seriality should be seen as a form. That is, a form according to Władysław Tatarkiewicz who claimed that a form is, among other things, an *arrangement of parts*. […] In this case the opposite or correlative of form are the elements, components or parts which form *A* unites or melds into a whole (1980: 220).

102 E.g. Busni (2015), Dunn (2005), Godzic (2004), Innocenti and Pescatore (2008), Grignaffini (2012).

103 The same may be said about such phenomena as quality TV (see e.g. McCabe and Akass 2011, Schlütz 2016), cult TV (see e.g. Abbott 2010, Gwenlian-Jones and Pearsons 2004, Lavery 2010) or specific sorts of TV series (e.g. Geraghty 1981).

104 E.g. *Don Matteo*.

At the same time, we would also like to suggest that seriality may be metaphorically said to be the medium of TV series.[105] As David Davies states:

> In its most general sense, a medium is a *means* of transmitting some matter or content from a source to a site of reception. The function of a medium, so construed, is *mediation*.
>
> DAVIES 2005: 181

Additionally, it is possible to distinguish the physical medium from the artistic one:

> In the case of paintings, for example, the physical medium consists of pigments (oils, tempera, water colours) applied to a surface (wood, canvas, glass), while the artistic medium is 'a purposeful system of brushstrokes'. Similarly, in talking about dance, the physical medium of bodily movements is to be distinguished from the artistic medium of articulated steps. While the artistic medium may be physically embodied, we must think of the work as made up not of physical elements as such but of elements like dance steps or brush-strokes that are 'informed by the purposiveness of the entire work'.
>
> DAVIES 2005: 183

We contend that seriality has an analogous role in TV series to the one played by the artistic medium in arts.[106] The televisual medium allows one to show a particular narrative, whereas seriality is an intentional manner of organizing what is shown thanks to the televisual medium in such a way as to make of it a serial whole.

Summing up, no one denies that it is possible to point out *differentiae specificae* of TV genres, deeming certain shows to be their standard embodiments and others their border cases, and the same is true in the case of seriality. Just as genre analysis does not really serve to qualify shows as belonging to a specific genre, so too an analysis of seriality does not aim at deciding which works are TV series, TV serials, or hybrid forms. If we claim that seriality involves normativity, our intention is neither to define any norms of seriality nor to declare what TV series should be like. We only claim that seriality as a cultural

---

105 A similar approach may be found in Bandirali and Terrone (2012: 18) who claim that "[being] divided into episodes and seasons, TV series are not a technological medium, but an artistic one, i.e. they are a specific system of representation and communication."

106 On television as medium see Cardwell (2014), Nannicelli (2016: 51–87).

phenomenon implies the existence of certain principles (conventions) in so far as creating and watching TV series are concerned. Of course, these principles do not have to be followed, but departing from them has consequences for what is created as a TV series and how it is experienced.

Is it possible to watch a single episode without considering it to be a part of a TV series? It is. Is it possible to watch a TV series "backwards"? It is. Is it possible to get aesthetic satisfaction in both cases? Beyond any doubt. It seems, however, that if we decide to watch them in accordance with the categorial norm our aesthetic satisfaction may be fuller, and we should endeavour to fulfil the aesthetic norm. A standard manner of watching a TV series or its parts allows one to better experience their formal and content richness. Looking at *Opałka 1965/∞* as a serial work opens more interpretational possibilities than dismissing its serial character. We may also ask whether it is possible to watch a TV series as if it were a super long film? Of course, it is, albeit in all likelihood many of its elements may appear pretty odd and as a result aesthetic satisfaction may be lessened.

As far as the second objection is concerned, we would like to underline that we, indeed, narrow the meaning of the term *seriality*. It is often used in a general way and as a result seriality turns out to be a family resemblance which does not explain a lot—what do Andy Warhol's cans have in common with Scheherazade's stories? What is more, although seriality is highly valued today, it still tends to be understood as based on repeatability and reproducibility.

Our approach to seriality stems from our belief that non-trivial seriality is particularly interesting from the point of view of philosophical aesthetics because it is distinct from all the other phenomena considered to be serial in one sense or another. What makes non-trivially serial works (let us remark, as an aside, that they do not have to be TV series even if for various economic and technological reason they are nowadays) so interesting is their cultural impact, which may be easily observed on a local as well as global scale.

We do not want to belittle other forms of seriality, assuming that non-trivial seriality at its "highest" level is a sort of pop-cultural avant-garde verging on art. On the contrary, we conceive of TV series as contemporary epitomes of popular culture which thus proves its creative potential. Being based on the dialectic of repetition and innovation, seriality as we understand it has little to do with seriality conceived of as a mere mechanical reproduction. The idea of non-trivial seriality may be, however, helpful in understanding a number of dissimilarities among serial works as well as how they all, in spite of their heterogeneousness, differ from works that are considered serial in so far as they are just copies of a given model as well as from non-serial works, no matter whether they are qualified as high culture or popular culture.

If we then want to associate seriality with normativity, we want to do it only inasmuch as it is possible to e.g. link the idea of making a painting with normativity. One may think of a theory of painting which defines what a standard painting looks like not in order to criticize certain pictures as falling short of this standard or to dismiss certain images as non-paintings, but to identify "paintings-beyond-painting" or paintings that are only "minimally" paintings. The issue of a standard manner of watching a TV series is to be approached in a similar way. For example, binge watching is not to be criticized on any ground, yet in order to even start describing this cultural phenomenon, one has to refer to some standard mode of reception as the one which is being transgressed (even if this standard mode is strictly personal, it usually refers to a standard implied by the TV series approached in a traditional way).

In other words, even if we have been living in an era when "personcasting" (Lotz 2014: 244]) makes "asynchronicity a defining feature of the post-network era" (ibid.: 245), which definitely changes the way TV series are created, distributed, and consumed, they are still non-trivially serial TV works. TV series are still produced as TV series and not as any other format, which means that their ontology is serial in character in spite of all the changes they have been undergone over the last two decades or so. As a result, it is possible to think that some ways of watching them are more aligned with their ontology than others in the sense that they take into account their non-trivial serial character to a greater extent. This does not mean, however, that such standard ways of watching TV series are per se better and as such are mandatory, even though it is reasonable to claim—as we do—that they allow one to get more of the aesthetic satisfaction implied by TV series. What is at stake here is rather the fact that if we want to maintain the idea of TV series as a distinct format, we have to conserve the concept of ontological non-trivial seriality together with its aesthetic ramifications at least as a point of reference. What would a TV series be without its serial character? Would there be any difference between watching a TV series and a TV film? For the time being, we do not really seriously raise these questions in circumstances other than academic, for we can easily distinguish TV series from other TV cinematic works. We discover their intended seriality and we adjust to it in one way or another, having a sort of tacit knowledge of their categorial and aesthetic norms.

Finally, as far as canon is concerned, we admit that we rely on it, but we treat all the TV series we mentioned only as examples of seriality that is not to be limited to supposedly canonical works and which can also be—and in fact is—present in "invisible television". At the same time, we cannot really deny that we are "acca/fans" fascinated by—as Buonanno (2013: 80) states—"narrative complexity, visual attractiveness, intertextuality, and cult qualities".

At the end, we would like to come back to the issue of aesthetics as criticism, by stating that TV series may be valued in many ways. For example, they may be compared to other TV series with the same genre, but one also can judge them internally in terms of overall complexity. What is more, this quality of a TV series may be its principal value, without which it would be rather dull. In other words, what makes some TV productions interesting or more noteworthy than others is not so much their content—which may consist of schematically reiterated well-known protagonists, motifs, events, etc.—as the way they are organized into wholes. It is their seriality that makes them so innovative in spite of all the repetitions identifiable in them.[107] In such cases seriality comes to the foreground and as a result what is mainly required from the viewers are skills allowing them to experience it. These are not aesthetic arcana, but abilities acquired through watching TV series.

More and more contemporary TV series are based on "serial outbidding" (Sudman 2017a, 2017b), i.e. on showing and playing with their serial character or—as we claim—with their seriality-based ontology. At the same time such shows imply viewers that are able to appreciate these effects, i.e. that they are capable of fulfilling the categorial norm and thus the aesthetic one. All this seems to be the best proof of the normativity implied by seriality; there is no doubt that there is a close relationship between law and TV series.

Bibliography

Abbott, Stacey, ed. 2010. *The Cult TV Book*. London: I.B. Tauris.

Allen, Rob and van der Berg, Thijs, eds. 2014. *Serialization in Popular Culture*. London: Routledge.

Allen, Robert C. 2001. "Introduction." In *To Be Continued: Soap Operas Around the World*, edited by Robert C. Allen, 1–26. London: Routledge.

Allrath, Gaby and Gymnich, Marion and Surkat, Carola. 2005. *Narrative Strategies in Television Series*, edited by Gaby Allrath and Marion Gymnich, 1–43. Houndmills: Palgrave Macmillan.

Andina, Tiziana. 2017a. "Normativity and Beauty in Contemporary Arts." *Rivista di estetica*, 64 (1): 151–66.

Andina, Tiziana. 2017b. "Contemporary Art: Judgments and Normativity." *Rivista di estetica*, 65 (2): 79–90.

Andina, Tiziana. 2017c. "What is Art? The Question of Definition Reloaded." *Brill Research Perspectives on Art and Law*, 1 (2): 1–88.

107 E.g. *Lost*.

Andrzejewski, Adam. 2015. "Framing Artification." *Estetika*, 52 (2): 131–151.

Aprile, Marcello. 2010. "La serialità televisiva. Uno sguardo complessivo." In Marcello Aprile and Debora de Fazio, *La serialità televisiva. Lingua e linguaggio nella fiction italiana e straniera*, 13–50. Galatina: Congedo.

Asimow, Michael, ed. 2009. *Lawyers in Your Living Room!: Law on Television*. Chicago (Ill.): American Bar Association.

Bandirali, Luca and Terrone, Enrico. 2012. *Filosofia delle serie TV: dalla scena del crimine al trono di spade*. Milano: Mimesis.

Bandirali, Luca and Terrone, Enrico. 2017. "Super Size Stories. Narrative Strategies in Contemporary TV Series", *Cinergie* 11, 98–110.

Bayard, Pierre. 2012. *How To Talk About Books You Haven't Read*. New York: Bloomsbury.

Beardsley, Monroe. 1958. *Aesthetics: Problems in the Philosophy of Criticism*. Harcourt, Brace & World.

Beil, Benjamin et al. 2012. "Einleitung in der Schwerpunkt." *Zeitschrift für Medienwissenschaften* 7 (2): 10–16.

Bell, Clive. 1914. *Art*. CreateSpace Independent Publishing Platform, [2015].

"Belphégore" 2016 14(1).

Ben Dor, Oren. 2012. *Law and Art: Justice, Ethics and Aesthetics*. London: Routledge.

Benjamin, Walter. 2008. "The Work of Art in the Age of Its Reproducibility." In Walter Benjamin, *The Work of Art in the Age of Its Technological Reproducibility, and Other Essays on Media*, 19–55. Cambridge (Mass.): Cambridge University Press.

Berger, Arthur Asa 1997. *Narratives in Popular Culture, Media, and Everyday Life*. Thousand Oaks–London–New Delhi: Sage Publishers.

Bocheński, Józef. M. 1965. "Analysis of Authority." In Józef M. Bocheński, *The Logic of Religion*. New York: New York University Press.

Bonazzi, Franco. 2001. *Televisione e serialità: il tempo ritrovato: l'offerta televisiva garantisce a ognuno il suo destino seriale?*. Milano: F. Angeli.

Booth, Paul. 2018, ed. *A Companion to Media Fandom and Fan Studies*. Wiley and Sons (e-book).

Bourdaa, Melanie. 2011. "Quality Television: Construction and De-construction of Seriality." In *Previously on ...*, edited by Miguel R. Perez-Gomez, 33–43. Sevilla: Universidad de Sevilla.

Brancato, Sergio (ed). 2011. *Post-serialità: per una sociologia delle tv-series: dinamiche di trasformazione della fiction televisiva*. Napoli: Liguori.

Brojakowski, Benjamin. 2015. "Spoiler Alert. Understanding Television Enjoyment in the Social Media Era." In *Television, Social Media, and Fan Culture*, edited by Alison Slade, Amber J. Narro, and Dedria Givens-Carroll, 23–42. Lanham (MD): Lexington Books.

Brożek, Anna. 2013. "Bocheński on Authority." *Studies in East European Thought*, 65 (1–2): 115–133.

Brożek, Bartosz. 2013b. *Rule-Following. From Imitation to the Normative Mind*. Kraków: Copernicus Center Press.

Brunsdon, Charlotte. 1997. *Screen Tastes: Soap Opera to Satellite Dishes*. London: Routledge.

Budd, Malcolm. 2003. "The Acquaintance Principle." *The British Journal of Aesthetics*, 43 (4): 386–392.

Buonanno, Milly. 2008. *Le formule del racconto televisivo: la sovversione del tempo nelle narrative seriali*. Firenze: Sansoni.

Buonanno, Milly. 2013. "La qualità della fiction fra tradizione nazionale e standards transnazionali." In *Tempo di fiction. Il racconto televisivo in divenire*, edited by Milly Buonanno, 71–87. Napoli: Liguore.

Busni, Simona. 2015. "The Genre Between Television and Cinema: for an Aesthetics of the Serialization." *Comunicazioni sociali* 2: 153–162.

"Cahiers de narratologie" 2016 31.

Calabrese, Omar. 1984. "I Replicanti." In *L'immagine al plurale. Serialità e ripetizione nel cinema e nella televisione*, edited by Francesco Casetti, 63–83. Venezia:, Marsilio.

Caldwell, John T. 1995. *Televisuality: Style, Crisis and Authority in American Television*. New Brunswick, NJ: Rutgers University Press.

Cardwell, Sarah. 2005. "Television Aesthetics and Close Analysis: Style, Mood and Engagement. In *Perfect Strangers* (Stephen Poliakoff, 2001)." In *Style and Meaning: Studies in the Detailed Analysis of Film*, edited by John Gibbs and Douglas Pye. Manchester: Manchester University Press.

Cardwell, Sarah. 2007. "Is Quality Television Any Good? Generic Distinctions, Evaluations and the Troubling Matter of Critical Judgement." In *Quality TV. Contemporary American Television and Beyond*, edited by Janet McCabe and Kim Akass. London and New York: I.B.Tauris.

Cardwell, Sarah. 2013. "Television Aesthetics: Stylistic Analysis and Beyond." In *Television, Aesthetics and Style*, edited by Jason Jacobs and Steven Peacock, 23–44. London: Bloomsbury.

Cardwell, Sarah. 2014. "Television Amongst Friends: Medium, Art, Media." *Critical Studies in Television* 9 (3): 6–21.

Carlson, Allen. 1981. "Nature, Aesthetic Judgment, and Objectivity." *The Journal of Aesthetics and Art Criticism*, 40 (1): 15–27.

Carlson, Allen. 1999. *Aesthetics and the Environment*. New York: Routledge.

Carneiro, Maria Francisca. 2011. "Law and Aesthetics." Accessed March 29, 2018. https://ssrn.com/abstract=1865905.

Carroll, Noël. 1998. *Philosophy of Mass Art*. Oxford: Oxford University Press.

Cavell, Stanley. 1984. *The World Viewed: Reflections of the Ontology of Film*. Harvard: Harvard University Press.

Chalmers, David J. 2011. "Verbal Disputes." *The Philosophical Review*, 120 (4): 515–566.

Chaplin, Tamara. 2017. *Turning On the Mind: French Philosophers on Television*. Chicago: University of Chicago Press.

Chatman, Seymour. 1978. *Story and Discourse. Narrative Structure in Fiction and Film*. Ithaca and London: Cornell University Press.

Click, Melissa and Scott, Suzanne, eds. 2017. *The Routledge Companion to Media Fandom*. New York: Routledge.

Cohen, Ted. 1993. "High and Low Thinking About High and Low Art." *The Journal of Aesthetics and Art Criticism*, 51 (2): 151–156.

Cook, Roy T. 2013. "Canonicity and Normativity in Massive, Serialized, Collaborative Fiction." *Journal of Art and Aesthetic Criticism* 71(3): 271–276.

Creeber, Glen. 2013. *Small Screen Aesthetics: from TV to the Internet*. Houndmills: Palgrave Macmillan.

Danto, Arthur C. 1981. *The Transfiguration of the Common Place: A Philosophy of Art*. Harvard: Harvard University Press.

Davies, David. 2004. *Art as Performance*. Oxford: Blackwell.

Davies, David. 2005. "Medium in Art." In *The Oxford Handbook of Aesthetics*, edited by Jerrold Levinson, 181–191. Oxford: Oxford University Press.

De George, Richard T. 1985. *The Nature and Limits of Authority*. Laurence, KS: University Press of Kansas.

Deleuze, Gilles. 2004. *Difference and Repetition*, translated by Paul Patton. London: Continuum.

Denson, Shan and Jahn-Sundman, Andreas. 2013. "Digital Seriality: on the Serial Aesthetics and Practice of Digital Games." *Eludamos* 7(1): 1–32.

Dowling, Christopher. 2010. "The Aesthetics of Daily Life." *The British Journal of Aesthetics*, 50 (3): 225–42.

Dunn, Anne. 2005. "The Genres of Television." In Helen Fulton, Rosemary Huisman, Julian Murphet, and Anne Dunn, *Narrative and Media*, 125–139. New York: Cambridge University Press.

Dusi, Nicola. 2016. "Seriality, Repetition and Innovation in Breaking Bad's Recaps and Teasers." *Cinergie* 10: 136–147.

Dyer, Jennifer. 2011. *Serial Images: The Modern Art of Iteration*. Wien: Lit Verlag.

Eder, Jens. 2010. "Understanding Characters." *Projections*, 4 (1): 16–40.

Eder, Jens, Fotis Jannidis, and Rolf Schneider, eds. 2010. *Characters in Fictional Worlds: Understanding Imaginary Beings in Literature, Film and Other Media*. Berlin: de Gruyter.

Eichner, Susanne, Lothar Mikos and Reiner Winter, eds. 2013. *Transnationale Serienkultur Theorie, Ästhetik, Narration und Rezeption neuer Fernsehserien*. Wiesbaden: Springer.

Ellis, John. 2001. *Visibile Fictions. Cinema, Television, Video*. London: Routledge.

Erickson, Hall. 2009. *Encyclopedia of Television Law Shows: Factual and Fictional Series about Judges, Lawyers and the Courtroom, 1948–2008*. Jefferson, N.C.: McFarland & Co.

Feuer, Jane, Paul Kerr, and Tise Vahimagi. 1984. MTM: "Quality Television". London: BFI.

Fish, Stanley. 1980. "How to Recognize a Poem When One Sees It." In Stanley Fish, *Is There a Text in This Class? The Authority of Interpretive Communities*, 322–337. Cambridge (Mass.): Cambridge University Press.

Fisher, John A. 2001. "High Art versus Low Art." In *The Routledge Companion to Aesthetics*, edited by Berys Gaut and Dominic Lopes. New York: Routledge.

Fiske, John. 1987. *Television Culture*. London and New York: Methuen.

Fulton, Hellen, Rosemary Huisman, Julian Murphet, and Anne Dunn. 2005. *Narrative and Media*. Cambridge: Cambridge University Press.

Garcìa, Alberto N. (2016). "A Storytelling Machine: The Complexity and Revolution of Narrative Television." *Between 11*. Accessed March, 29, 2018. http://www.betweenjournal.it.

Gearey, Adam. 2001. *Law and Aesthetics*. Portland (Or.): Hart.

Geraghty, Christine. 1981. "Continous Serial—a Definition." In *Coronation Street*, edited by Richard Dyer, 9–26. London: British Film Institute.

Geraghty, Christine. 2003. "Aesthetics and Quality in Popular Television." *International Journal of Cultural Studies*, 6 (1): 25–45.

Geraghty, Lincoln. 2015. *Popular Media Cultures: Fans, Audiences and Paratexts*. Houndmills: Palgrave Macmillan.

Godzic, Wiesław. 2004. *Telewizja i jej gatunki. Po "Wielkim Bracie"*. Kraków: Universitas.

Golubiewski, Mikołaj, Adam Andrzejewski, and Joanna Kulas. 2014. "Everyday Aesthetics of Popular Culture: *Dexter*'s Opening Sequence." In *Aesthetics of Popular Culture* edited by Jozef Kovalcik and Max Ryynanen. Bratislava: SlovArt Press.

Goodman, Nelson. 1968. *Languages of Art*. Indianapolis (In.): Hackett Publishing Company Inc.

Grasso, Aldo. 2007. *Buona maestra. Perchè i telefilm sono diventati piu importanti del cinema e dei libri*. Milano: Mondadori.

Grignaffini, Giorgio. 2012. *I generi televisivi*. Roma: Carocci.

Grispund, Jostein. 1995. *The Dynasty Years: Hollywood, Television and Critical Media Studies*. London: Routledge.

Gwenllian-Jones, Sara and Roberta E. Pearsons. 2004. "Introduction." In *Cult TV*, edited by Sara Gwenllian-Jones and Roberta E. Pearsons, IX–XX. Minneapolis (Mn.): University of Minnesota Press.

Haak, Susan. 2005. "On Legal Pragmatism. Where Does 'The Path of the Law' Lead Us?" *American Journal of Jurisprudence*, 50 (1): 71–105.

Hills, Matt. 2002. *Fan Cultures*. London: Routledge 2002.

Hills, Matt. 2004. "Defining Cult TV. Texts, Inter-texts and Fan Audiences" In *The Television Studies Reader*, edited by Robert C. Allen and Annette, 509–523. London: Routledge.

"History of Science" 2010 48 (3–4).

Horrowitz, Nancy. 1984. "The Body of the Detective Model: Charles S. Peirce and Edgar Allan Poe." In *The Sigh of Three: Dupin, Holmes, Perice*, edited by Umberto Eco and Thomas Sebeok, 179–197 Bloomington: Indiana University Press.

Horvath, Jared C. et al. 2016. "The Impact of Binge Watching on Memory and Perceived Comprehension." First Monday 22 (9). Accessed March 29, 2018. http://dx.doi.org/10.5210/fm.v22i19.7729.

Hutter, Albert. 1983. "Dreams, Transformations, and Literature: The Implications of Detective Fiction." In *The Poetics of Murder: Detective Fiction and Literary Theory*, edited by Glenn W. Most, and William W. Stowe, New York: Harcourt Brace Jovanovich.

Ingarden, Roman. 1973. *The Cognition of the Literary Work of Art*. Translated by G.G. Grabowicz. Evnston: Northwesten University Press.

Innocenti, Veronica and Guglielmo Pescatore. 2008. *Le nuove forme della serialità televisiva: storia, linguaggio e temi*. Bologna: Archetipolibri.

Irvin, Sherri. 2005. "Artist's Sanction in Contemporary Art." *The Journal of Aesthetics and Art Criticism* 63 (4): 283–304.

Jacobs, Jason and Steven Peacock, eds. 2013. *Television, Aesthetics and Style*. London: Bloomsbury.

Jacobs, Jason. 2000. *The Intimate Screen: Early British Television Drama*. Oxford: Oxford University Press.

Jacobs, Jason. 2001. "Issues of Judgement and Value in Television Studies." *International Journal of Cultural Studies* 4(4): 427–447.

Jenner, Mareike. 2017. "Binge-watching: Video-on-demand, Quality TV and Mainstreaming Fandom." *International Journal of Cultural Studies* 20(3): 304–320.

Kant, Immanuel. 1790. *Critique of Judgment*. Translated by James Creed Meredith. Oxford: Oxford University Press [1928].

Keinonen, Heidi. 2016. "From Serial Drama to Transmedia Storytelling: How to Re-articulate Television Aesthetics in the Post-broadcast Era." *Northern Lights* 14: 65–81.

Kelleter, Frank, ed. 2012. *Populäre Serialität: Narration–Evolution–Distinktion. Zum seriellen Erzählen seit dem 19. Jahrhundert*. Bielefeld: Transcript Verlag.

Kelleter, Frank, ed. 2017. *Media of Serial Narrative*. Columbus (Oh.): Ohio State University Press.

Klein, Amanda Ann and R. Barton Palmer, eds. 2016, *Cycles, Sequels, Spin-offs, Remakes, and Reboots Multiplicities in Film and Television*. Austin (Tx.): Austin University Press.

Kozloff, Sarah. 2005. "Narrative Theory and Television." In *Channels of Discourse, Reassembled. Television and Contemporary Criticism*, edited by Robert C. Allen, 52–76. New York: Routledge.

Krauss, Rosalind. 1986. "The Originality of Avant-garde." In Rosalind Krauss, *The Originality of the Avant-garde and Other Modernist Myths*, 151–170. Boston (Mass.): The MIT Press.

Kustritz, Anne. 2014. "Seriality and Transmediality in the Fan Multiverse: Flexible and Multiple Narrative Structures in Fan Fiction, Art, and Vids." *TV/Series* 4. Accessed March 29, 2018. http://tvseries.revues.org/331.

Laetz, Brian. 2010. "Kendall Walton's 'Categories of Art': A Critical Commentary." *The British Journal of Aesthetics*, 50 (3): 287–306.

Lamarque, Peter. 2010. *Art & Object: Explorations in the Metaphysics of Art*. Oxford: Oxford University Press.

Lavery, David, ed. 2010. *Essential Cult TV Reader*. Lexington: University Press of Kentucky.

Leddy, Tom. 2012. "Aesthetization, Artification, and Aquariums." *Contemporary Aesthetics*, special issue 4. Accessed March 29, 2018. https://contempaesthetics.org/newvolume/pages/article.php?articleID=643.

Letourneux, Matthieu. 2017. *Fictions à la chaîne: littératures sérielles et culture médiatique*. Paris: Éditions du Seuil.

Levine, Lawrence W. 1988. *Highbrow/Lowbrow: The Emergence of Cultural Hierarchy in America*. Cambridge, Mass: Harvard University Press.

Levinson, Jerrold. 2003. "Philosophical Aesthetics: An Overview." In *The Oxford Handbook of Aesthetics*, edited by Jerrold Levinson, 3–24. Oxford: Oxford University Press.

Lopes, Dominic. 2015. "Aesthetic Experts, Guides to Value." *The Journal of Aesthetics and Art Criticism*, 73 (3): 234–246.

Lotz, Amanda. 2014. *The Television Will be Revolutionized*. New York: New York University Press.

Lukes, Steven. 1978. "Power and Authority." In *A History of Sociological Analysis*, edited by Tom Bottomore and Robert Nisbet, 633–676. London: Heinemann.

Mag Uidhir, Christy. 2013. "How to Frame Serial Art." *The Journal of Aesthetics and Art Criticism* 71 (3): 261–265.

Manovich, Lev. 2017. "Aesthetics, 'Formalism,' and Media Studies." In *Keywords for Media Studies*, edited by Jonathan Gray and Laurie Ouellette, 9–12. New York: New York University Press.

Margolis, Joseph. 2010. *What, After All, Is a Work of Art?: Lectures in the Philosophy of Art*. Pennsylvania: Penn State University Press.

Marmor, Andrei. 2011. "The Conventional Foundations of Law." In *New Essays on the Normativity of Law*, edited by Stefano Bertea and George Pavlakos, Oxford: Hart Publishing, 143–157.

McCabe, Janet and Kim Akass, eds. 2011. *Quality TV: Contemporary American Television and Beyond*. London: I.B. Tauris.

Melchionne, Kevin. 2013. "The Definition of Everyday Aesthetics." *Contemporary Aesthetics*, volume 11. Accessed March 29, 2018. https://contempaesthetics.org/newvolume/pages/article.php?articleID=663%20.

Metallinos, Nikos. 1996. *Television Aesthetics: Perceptual, Cognitive and Compositional Bases*. Mahwah (NJ): Lawrence Erlbau Associates.

Mills, Brett. 2010. "Invisible Television: The Programmes No-One Talks about Even Though Lots of People Watch Them." *Critical Studies in Television* 5 (1): 1–16.

Mittell, Jason. 2006. "Narrative Complexity in Contemporary American Television." *Velvet Light Trap*, 29–40.

Mittell, Jason. 2013. "The Qualities of Complexity: Vast versus Dense Seriality in Contemporary Television." In *Television Aesthetics and Beyond*, edited by Steven Peacock and Jason Jacobs. London: Bloomsbury.

Mittell, Jason. 2014. "Strategies of Storytelling on Transmedia Television." In *Storyworlds accross Media*, edited by Marie-Laure Ryan and Jan-Noel Thorn.

Mittell, Jason. 2015. *Complex TV the Poetics of Contemporary Television Storytelling*. New York: New York University Press.

Morgan, Ed. 2007. *The Aesthetics of International Law*. Toronto: University of Toronto Press.

Mothersill, Mary. 1984. *Beauty Restored*. Oxford: Clarendon Press.

Nannicelli, Ted. 2012. "Ontology, Intentionality and Television Aesthetics." *Screen*, 53 (2): 164–179.

Nannicelli, Ted. 2016. *Appreciating the Art of Television: A Philosophical Perspective*. London: Routledge.

Naukkarinen, Ossi. 2012. "Variations in Artification." *Contemporary Aesthetics*, special issue 4. Accessed March 29, 2018. https://contempaesthetics.org/newvolume/pages/article.php?articleID=635.

Naukkarinen, Ossi. 2017. "Everyday Aesthetics and Everyday Behavior." *Contemporary Aesthetics*, volume 15. Accessed March 29, 2018. https://contempaesthetics.org/newvolume/pages/article.php?articleID=802.

Novitz, David. 1992. *The Boundaries of Art*. Philadelphia: Temple University Press.

Oltean, Tudor. 1993. "Series and Seriality in Media Culture." *European Journal of Communication*, 8 (5): 5–31.

Parsons, Glenn. 2002. "Nature Appreciation, Science, and Positive Aesthetics." *The British Journal of Aesthetics*, 42 (3): 279–295.

Parsons, Glenn. 2006. "Freedom and Objectivity in the Aesthetic Appreciation of Nature." *The British Journal of Aesthetics*, 46 (1): 17–37.

Pearson, Roberta. 2008. "Chain of Events: Regimes of Evaluation and *Lost*'s Construction of the Televisual Character." In *Reading "Lost"*. Edited by Roberta Pearson. London: I.B. Tauris. 139–158.

Pratt, Henry John. 2013. "Why Serials Are Killers." *Journal of Art and Aesthetic Criticism* 71(3): 266–270.

Ratiu, Dan. E. 2013. "Remapping the Realm of Aesthetics: On Recent Controversies About the Aesthetics and Aesthetic Experience in Everyday Life." *Estetika*, 50 (1): 3–26.

Reymer, Mavis, Nyala Ali, Deanna England and Melanie Dennis Unrau, eds. 2014. *Seriality and Texts for Young People: The Compulsion to Repeat*. Houndmills: Palgrave Macmillan.

Robson, Peter and Jennifer L. Schulz *A Transnational Study of Law and Justice on TV*. Portland (Or.): Hart Publishing.

Roman Opałka. 1999. München: Prestel.

Ryynanen, Max. 2005. "Nobrow." *The Nordic Journal of Aesthetics*, 32 (1):86–98.

Saito, Yuriko. 2012. "Everyday Aesthetics and Artification." *Contemporary Aesthetics*, special issue 4. Accessed March 29, 2018. https://contempaesthetics.org/newvolume/pages/article.php?articleID=640.

Schachek, Sarah. 2013 *Pornography and Seriality: The Culture of Producing Pleasure*. New York: Palgrave Macmillan.

Schleich, Markus and Jonas Nesselhauf. 2016. *Fernsehserien: Geschichte, Theorie, Narration*. Tübingen: A. Francke Verlag.

Schlütz, Daniela. 2016. *Quality-TV als Unterhaltungsphänomen*. Wiesbaden: Springer Verlag.

Shuster, Martin. 2017. *New Television: The Aesthetics and Politics of a Genre*. Chicago (Ill.): University of Chicago Press.

Shusterman, Richard. 1991. "Form and Funk: The Aesthetic Challenge of Popular Art." *The British Journal of Aesthetics*, 31 (3): 203–213.

Shusterman, Richard. 2003. "Entertainment: A Question for Aesthetics." *The British Journal of Aesthetics* 43 (3): 289–307.

Sibley, Frank. 1965. "Aesthetic and Nonaesthetic." *The Philosophical Review*, 74 (2): 135–159.

Slowinska, Maria A. 2014. *Art/Commerce: The Convergence of Art and Marketing in Contemporary Culture*. Bielefeld: Transcript Verlag.

Smith, Murray. 1995. *Engaging Characters: Fiction, Emotion and the Cinema*. New York: Oxford University Press.

Stevanovic, Melisa. 2013. *Deontic Rights in Interaction. A Conversation Analytic Study on Authority and Cooperation*. Doctoral Thesis. University of Helsinki.

Sudman, Andreas. 2017a. "Watching *Lost* and Experiencing Outbidding (Überbietung) as a Serial Form." In *Lost in Media*, edited by Benjamin Beil, Herbert Schwaab and Daniela Wentz, 97–116. Münster: Lit Verlag.

Sudmann, Andreas. 2017b. *Serielle Überbietung. Zur televisuellen Ästhetik und Philosophie exponierter Steigerungen*. Stuttgart: J.B. Metzler Verlag.

Tatarkiewicz, Władysław. 1980. *A History of Six Ideas. An Essay in Aesthetics*. The Hague–Warsaw: Martinus Nijhof, Polskie Wydawnictwo Naukowe.

Thomansson, Amie L. 2005. "The Ontology of Art and Knowledge in Aesthetics." *The Journal of Aesthetics and Art Criticism*, 63 (3): 221–229.

Thompson, Kristin. 2003. *Storytelling in Film and Television*. Cambridge (Mass.): Cambridge University Press.

Thompson, Robert, J. 1997. *Television's Second Golden Age: From Hill Street Blues to ER*, Syracuse University Press.

Thorburn, David. 1987. "Television as an Aesthetic Medium." *Critical Studies in Mass Communication* 4: 161–173.

Ulrich, Anne and Joachim Knape. 2014. *Medienrhetorik des Fernsehens: Begriffe und Konzepte*. Bielefeld: Transcript Verlag.

Vidmar, Iris. 2017. "Fictional Characters." In *Perspectives on the Self*, edited by Boran Beri, 303–328. Rijeka: University of Rijeka Press.

Villez, Barbara. 2009. *Television and the Legal System*. London: Routledge.

Walton, Douglas. 1997. *Appeal to Expert Opinion: Arguments from Authority*. University Park, PA: Pennsylvania University Press.

Walton, Kendall. 1970. "Categories of Art." *The Philosophical Review*, 79 (3): 334–367.

Watson, Jamie Carlin and Robert Arp. 2011. *What's Good on TV?: Understanding Ethics Through Television*. Oxford: John Wiley and Sons.

Weiss, Jennifer. 2014. *Clue, Code, Conjure: The Epistemology of American Detective Fiction, 1841–1914*. New York: CUNY. Doctoral dissertation.

Weitz, Morris. 1956. "The Role of Theory in Aesthetics." *The Journal of Aesthetics and Art Criticism* 15(1): 27–35.

Wells-Lassagne, Shannon. 2017. *Television and Serial Adaptation*. London: Routledge.

Welsch, Welsch. 1995. "Aesthetics Beyond Aesthetics." In *Proceedings of the XIIIth International Congress of Aesthetics*, edited by Martti Honkanen, 18–37. Helsinki: University of Helsinki.

Williams, Rebecca. 2015. *Post-Object Fandom: Television, Identity and Self-narrative*. New York: Bloomsbury.

Zangwill, Nick. 2003/2014. "Aesthetic Judgment." *Stanford Encyclopedia of Philosophy*, edited by Edward Zalta. Accessed March 29, 2018. https://plato.stanford.edu/archives/fall2014/entries/aesthetic-judgment.

Zborowski, James. 2016. "Television Aesthetics, Media and Cultural Studies and the Contested Realm of the Social." *Critical Studies in Television* 11(1): 7–22.

Zhou, Yanha. 2015. "Rethinking Seriality in Minimalist Art Practices." *Canadian Social Science* 7(11): 148–154.

Internet Sources

http://blog.commarts.wisc.edu/category/columns/the-aesthetic-turn/
http://heymancenter.org/events/the-new-seriality-studies
http://researchseries.squarespace.com
http://www.popsophia.it
http://www.popularseriality.de
https://www.uni-saarland.de/lehrstuhl/solte-gresser/forschung/serial-narration/home.html

www.ingramcontent.com/pod-product-compliance
Lightning Source LLC
Chambersburg PA
CBHW031333230926
51848CB00001B/216
9789004387874